Looking at Cuba

Contemporary Cuba Series

Florida A&M University, Tallahassee
Florida Atlantic University, Boca Raton
Florida Gulf Coast University, Ft. Myers
Florida International University, Miami
Florida State University, Tallahassee
University of Central Florida, Orlando
University of Florida, Gainesville
University of North Florida, Jacksonville
University of South Florida, Tampa
University of West Florida, Pensacola

Looking at Cuba

Essays on Culture and Civil Society

———

Rafael Hernández

Translated by Dick Cluster

University Press of Florida

Gainesville · Tallahassee · Tampa · Boca Raton
Pensacola · Orlando · Miami · Jacksonville · Ft. Myers

First English language edition. Originally published in Spanish as *Mirar a Cuba: Ensayos sobre cultura y sociedad civil* by Editorial Letras Cubanas, Havana, Cuba, 1999.

Printed in the United States of America on acid-free paper

08 07 06 05 04 03   6 5 4 3 2 1

Library of Congress Cataloging-in-Publication Data
Hernández, Rafael.
[Mirar a Cuba. English]
Looking at Cuba: essays on culture and civil society / Rafael Hernández; translated by Dick Cluster—1st English language ed.
p. cm. — (Contemporary Cuba)
Includes bibliographical references.
ISBN 0-8130-2642-3 (cloth: alk. paper)
1.Civil society—Cuba. 2. Cuba—Politics and government—1959–.
I. Title. II. Series.
JL1010.H4713   2003
300'.97291—dc21   2003054075

The University Press of Florida is the scholarly publishing agency
for the State University System of Florida, comprising Florida A&M
University, Florida Atlantic University, Florida Gulf Coast University,
Florida International University, Florida State University, University
of Central Florida, University of Florida, University of North Florida,
University of South Florida, and University of West Florida.

University Press of Florida
15 Northwest 15th Street
Gainesville, FL 32611–2079
http://www.upf.com

Contents

Foreword

John M. Kirk, Series Editor

It is easy to fall into the trap of complacency when studying Cuba. After all, what else is there to say? Studies galore have been written about that small island (population 11 million), and there is a veritable industry of works on "Cubanology." One voice is consistently missing from this plethora of voices, however, and particularly deserves our attention. Too often North American and European—and to a lesser extent Latin American—perspectives are presented as the only meaningful interpretation of events on that island. Conspicuously absent is the voice of the Cubans themselves.

Perhaps we feel that they don't really understand; or that they will merely parrot revolutionary dogma; or perhaps that they are afraid of speaking their minds for fear of government reprisal. While there may be some truth in this—certainly academics in other countries are often not keen to bite the hand that feeds them—the attitude reveals a superiority complex that is rather lamentable. With our media mostly clinging in a paternalistic fashion to voices from outside Cuba, the end result is that we rarely heed the observations of Cubans who choose to live, and do research, on the island.

We also fall into the unfortunate habit of dividing Cubans into simplistic groupings, largely revolving around a polarization of officialist fidelista versus dissident activist interpretations. Culture, we are informed by sources outside the island, is totally controlled by the government, and therefore horribly unrepresentative of popular aspirations.

And of course civil society—as seen from the West, or rather the North—is virtually nonexistent. Instead Cuba is a totalitarian dictatorship whose population unquestioningly do the bidding of *el comandante en jefe*.

As the present collection of essays by Rafael Hernández illustrates, this interpretation is both simplistic and wrong. Here we find the balanced analysis of a vibrant national culture, and a civil society that has been decades in the making. (Should there be any doubt concerning some slavish obedience to official cultural paradigms, one has only to view such films as *Strawberry and Chocolate, Guantanamera, The Waiting List, Madagascar,* and *Life Is to Whistle,* or to read the works of Leonardo Padura or Miguel Mejides or even Abel Prieto, Cuba's minister of culture, or to listen to the lyrics of *timba.*) Critical thinking is alive and well on the island.

North American commentators and politicians might bluster at Cuba's never-changing authoritarianism and rigid dogmatism, yet they miss the point, at times deliberately so. For beneath the surface a significant evolution has taken place in the Cuba of the "special period." The demise of the Soviet Union has, paradoxically, been extremely helpful in promoting a more open cultural expression, one that is the envy of Latin America.

These initial years of the millennium are very different indeed from the 1960s, and in this regard the observations of Hernández are instructive. Cuba has seen dramatic changes since the Soviet implosion, and they have brought with them considerations of the meaning of civil society. One of Cuba's top political analysts, Rafael Hernández comes from the tradition that is, in the words of Jorge Luis Acanda, "not only revolutionary but also autonomous, critical, and organic." His is a voice that we badly need to listen attentively to if we are, finally, to pay attention to an often ignored piece of the complex Cuban puzzle. Thoughtful, provocative, polemical—but absolutely necessary if we are to appreciate the "big picture" of life in Cuba today.

The value of these concise, superbly crafted essays of Rafael Hernández lies in their ability to engage readers, obliging them to step outside traditionally held views. The collection spotlights the need to seek balance, to demythify, and to revisit the paradigms that we have used for decades—often incorrectly—to evaluate the Cuban Revolution. Cuba, notes Hernández, is not "an island whose thinking population have all taken up residence abroad." We must be rigorously honest in our intellectual analysis, and also to strip away prejudgments. This book is a good place to start.

Foreword

Jorge Domínguez
Weatherhead Center for International Affairs, Harvard University

Looking at Cuba seeks to provoke a debate about interpretation of Cuba's past and Cuba's future. It is itself a part of that debate. At issue is how to "see" the Cuba that actually has existed since revolutionary victory in 1959 and, specifically, how to understand the nature of its civil society.

For some, mainly for those who look at Cuba from the United States, for many decades something called Cuban civil society has for the most part not existed. In this view, the Cuban government has suppressed the autonomy of Cuban civil society, shredding its foundations and reducing its significance. Only openly dissident intellectuals, activists, or their organizations, perhaps alongside communities of religious faith, may merit the label "civil society actors." Yet, according to this perspective, the openly dissident are very few and suffer persecution from the state, while the openly religious remain too few still.

For others, mainly within the Cuban regime's establishment, civil society exists, but only within the official network of organizations tasked with linking the state, the party, and the society. A report on the state of the nation, issued by the Central Committee of the Communist Party, articulated this view most clearly in March 1996. General Castro read a report on the state of the nation before the Central Committee of the Cuban Communist Party. A key portion of the report focused on the political significance of civil society in Cuba. Its definition of the country's civil society was limited to the official mass organizations sponsored by the government and the Communist Party, encompassing groups of workers, women, peasants, and artists, among others.

For the first set, therefore, Cuba's civil society is principally part of a future yet to be created. For the second set, Cuba's civil society is exclusively part of a past still to be defended. For Rafael Hernández, Cuban civil society is part of the present, born of a past that predates the revolution and was transformed by it, and evolving without a preset blueprint toward the future. Hernández's notion of Cuban civil society is thus far broader, suppler, and subtler than either the foreign or the officialist view would have it.

Hernández offers two main arguments about civil society in Cuba, the first addressed ostensibly to foreigners but indirectly, and more importantly, to fellow Cubans: The author takes issue with the common foreign assumption that the Cuban government suppresses civil society's autonomy and that only the overt political or religious dissident might qualify as a civil society actor. To the contrary, Hernández contends that Cuban civil society has endured—although its autonomy and independence have varied significantly over time—and that Cuba's community of nondissident intellectuals remains among its most significant components. Civil society in Cuba does indeed include officially sponsored organizations, although it is not limited to them. Hernández also notes that intellectuals are usually lawful participants in the civil arena who seek to reshape the contours of Cuban public life. Cuba's intellectuals, research shows, tend to support political decentralization, economic efficiency, more democratic political institutions, and struggles against religious, ethnic, or gender discrimination—a social and political agenda that would resonate with reformers around the world.

Yet Hernández acknowledges that the political influence of Cuba's intellectuals remains severely limited. He writes that the national political leadership largely determines the scope of the country's intellectual debates "in areas ranging from the reinterpretation of Cuban history to ideas about . . . revolutionary culture." The result has been "to rigidify cultural life and restrict the reproduction of ideas." Cuba's leading contemporary thinkers, therefore, have had little impact on public opinion. Hernández regards this outcome as a genuine loss, not only for Cuba's intellectual life but also for the health of the socialist regime. Cuban intellectuals participate in regime-sponsored institutions and display high levels of political commitment, "though they are also strongly critical of procedures that rein in the spirit of creative work and encourage such negative phenomena as inefficiency, mediocrity, fraud, and hypocrisy."

Hernández's message for Cuban citizens is that their civil society can be an agent of change and not inimical to a socialist regime. At the same time, he calls on foreigners to respect forms of expression and change within Cuba and to avoid counterproductive behavior that would in fact assist the hard-liners.

Empirical research on Cuba buttresses Hernández's principal arguments. Cuban civil society entities, including the more independent community organizations, do not promote antiregime activities but rather raise issues that can compel the government to alter its behavior. However, these entities are fragile; their weakness is exacerbated by the mistrust of some state officials. Were these state officials not a barrier, the participatory, problem-solving actions of each organization could serve socialism in Cuba and its government well. As it is, government bureaucracies are often an obstacle to civil society's democratizing endeavors.

Hernández wrote this book as a set of independent articles focusing on, and building upon, common themes. He wrote it as a participant in a debate regarding the standing of the civil society question in contemporary Cuba. By publishing the pieces in various Cuban journals, Hernández sought to stimulate discussions among Cuban socialists, including but not limited to his fellow Communist Party members, but also more generally among Cuban intellectuals independent of their political preferences.

Hernández's role as an engaged intellectual, defending Cuban foreign policy but also critically assessing aspects of state-society relations in Cuba, was not bereft of political significance. During his professional career, Hernández has at times been denied visas by the U.S. government because it deemed him too close to the Cuban government. And in the same March 1996 party report referred to above, certain Cuban think tanks—particularly the Centro de Estudios sobre América (Center for American Studies or CEA)—were denounced for allegedly echoing "inappropriate" foreign conceptions of civil society and democracy. Hernández was a prominent leader among the CEA intellectuals who were criticized; he and they had to leave the CEA and find employment elsewhere in Cuba. They were not ostracized, however; most of their writings are still published in Cuban magazines despite their way of looking at Cuba, a Cuba larger than the state and the Communist Party.

Cuba's civil society continues to grow and evolve, even as citizens attempt to expand public freedoms. The Cuban intellectual debate on civil society persists as well. This book's Spanish language version was published in Havana three years after that party report was made public. The likely outcome of the debate between the past and the future will probably be neither a stridently antiregime civil society nor one limited to official state-sponsored organizations. Instead, Cuba's civil society is becoming more genuine and less predictable, emphasizing the goals of local communities, not the fantasies and fears of government elites within and outside Cuba.

And Rafael Hernández, one of Cuba's premier intellectuals today, has illuminated and will continue to illuminate the ways of looking at his Cuba.

An earlier, different version of this essay was published as "An Increasingly Civil Cuba," *Foreign Policy,* September–October 2000, pp. 100, 102. It is reprinted here with permission.

Preface and Acknowledgments

The essays assembled in this volume were written as a contribution to a process of reflection about culture, politics, and society in Cuba. They have been collected here with the goal of presenting a modest personal example of the debate that has characterized Cuban social thought since the 1990s.

Chapters 2, 3, and 4 appeared between 1993 and 1994 in *La Gaceta de Cuba,* a cultural publication of the Writers' and Artists' Union, and were written to take a position in a debate about Cuba whose principal origin is from outside the island. The style and focus of these articles correspond to the confrontational dynamic from which they sprang. They are "think pieces," not academic studies. They make direct reference to works, authors, and visions of Cuban national reality put forward by foreigners (and also by Cubans) in recent years.

"Looking at Cuba," which extends its name to that of the whole book, attempts to refute a series of stereotyped images of Cuban intellectuals, leadership, political processes, and real society. This text had the good fortune to be among those that initiated a reflection from the perspective of Cuban civil society, conceived as a constructive angle of vision from which to examine the relations between culture and politics.

The next two essays take the texts of other authors as their points of departure. "Civil Society and Its Surroundings" was a response to the Cuban writer Armando Cristóbal's critical commentary on "Looking at Cuba," also published in *La Gaceta,* which questioned the use and meaning of the concept of civil society as applied to Cuban reality. "The Second Death of Dogma" was my critical response to the book *Utopia Unarmed* by the Mexican Jorge Castañeda; it begins with a discussion of the outlook of the Cuban and Latin American left and continues by examining the relationship between politics and intellectuals within socialism.

The text of chapter 5, "Civil Society and Politics in the 1990s," served originally as a presentation in 1995 in Havana at the Higher Institute of International Relations, in which I attempted to evaluate the concept in concrete application to Cuban politics and regional foreign relations.

"Toward a New Socialist Society?" originally appeared in the Venezuelan journal *Nueva Sociedad* in 1998, in response to an invitation from that magazine to discuss Cuban economic and political processes of the most recent years. Starting from a portrait of the new social actors, I tried to locate these processes in a regional and international context and to explain their significance for the current and future shape of the socialist system in Cuba—seen not only as a political system but also as a social and cultural formation.

"On Discourse," published in *La Gaceta* early in 1999, centers on considerations of culture, communication, and politics as seen from the perspective of civil society. My central preoccupation in this essay is not only to consider the effects of the transition in the subjective sphere of language but also to put the question of hegemony on the table. The text that closes this volume, "Three Cubans Talking Baseball," responds to the same challenge. Written after the publication of the first Cuban edition of *Looking at Cuba* and published in the winter 2001 issue of the Mexican magazine *Nexos*, this brief essay tries to depict the current debate over ideas in Cuba as it takes place in its major sites of dissemination, the cultural publications and social studies magazines on the island, which are in turn sounding boards for new thinking that is emerging in institutions and organizations of Cuban civil society.

The photos in this book mirror Cuban society during the crisis years and beyond. Photographers from different generations and artistic backgrounds, Rolando Pujol, Enrique de la Uz, Humberto Mayol, and Raúl Cañibano, grasp masterfully the daily-life drama, hardships, and fun experienced by ordinary Cubans. Their work shows a controversial, authentic, and compassionate view of Cuban society, urban as well as rural, that could be usefully contrasted with other images pretending to portray the "real Cuba." I wish to thank them and my old friend, artist José Manuel Fors, for their generosity in letting me use their photos in this book, as well as Lourdes Socarrás and Rufino del Valle, director and photography historian at the Fototeca de Cuba, for their support and guidance.

I would like, here at the beginning of the volume, to offer a warning about two risks. The first is the one I assume by assembling these essays here as if they were finished products, when they are actually shaped by a debate that itself completes them. The second is that these texts, conditioned by controversies in Cuba since the 1990s, are the result of a progression, not of any systematization; therefore a reader may encounter successive approximations of an issue that is difficult to grasp, and may find that these approximations do not jell into a single assessment.

I have decided to assume those risks, in the first place because I think that these writings (whatever their own merits may be) can serve as evidence about the *agency* of current Cuban thought—about its existence not only as thinking but as a kind of action—and in the second place because, as the reader may see, I am less interested in theoretical definitions of "civil society" than in its analytical uses, especially in the type of approach toward politics and culture with which it may provide us.

My thanks are due to those who encouraged these works and offered criticism of their earlier drafts, in particular to Graziella Pogolotti, Abel Prieto, Norberto Codina, Sheryl Lutjens, Armando Cristóbal, Nelson Valdés, Armando Hart, and Marisel Caraballo. I would also like to acknowledge the contributions of Jorge Luis Acanda and Jorge Domínguez, who first published (in Cuba and in the United States, respectively) insightful critical reviews of the Cuban edition of *Looking at Cuba*.

This edition in English has benefited from a wonderful translation by Dick Cluster, who, thanks to his knowledge of Cuban literary and popular culture, has improved the clarity and stylistic precision of the original texts wherever possible, as well as offering some crucial explanations for the Northamerican reader. Funding for the translation was provided by the Social Science Research Council.

This book is dedicated to Hugo Azcuy, prematurely gone, who acted with equal courage and lucidity in the fields of intellectual work and politics. I was lucky enough to have him read and enrich the majority of these essays in draft form, while he himself carried out a leading role in this debate in the 1990s, writing some of the most illuminating pages on Cuban civil society.

Naturally, I am the only one responsible for the content I have presented here, which I expect to have the opportunity to correct in the future.

Rafael Hernández, El Vedado, Havana, autumn 2001

I

Introduction

An Indiscreet Glance, or the Risks of a Window

Jorge Luis Acanda González

History tells us of a Frenchman at the turn of the twentieth century who, inspired by a desire to seek his own truth, had recourse to the unexpected expedient of a long sea voyage. He made this voyage, not in order to discover new lands, but to discover himself. He decided to write a book narrating his impressions—not of the geography that he would encounter, but of a fictional reality that he would invent in order to understand his spirit. This unclassifiable Frenchman (a great writer for some, for others simply a nut) set sail in a steamship for Australia and New Zealand, adopting a procedure as outlandish as his goal. He obstinately refused to go up on deck to see the scenery. He shut himself in his cabin to write. Because the porthole of his cabin represented an obstacle to introspection, he closed the curtains, nailing them in place to close off any view of the outside. Finally, in 1910, with the notes he had taken on this strange voyage, Raymond Roussel (for that was his name) published a book paradoxically titled *Impressions of Africa.*

At the end of the twentieth century, a Cuban decided to discover his country's reality, so as to know his own. In contrast to some of his countrymen, he did not decide to change places, to change his geographic point of residence, but to undertake an intellectual voyage. This Cuban, likewise unclassifiable (political scientist, sociologist, editor, poet, short story writer, and—the accidents of history—university graduate in the field of French literature) did not invent a reality, but decided to look at the real Cuba. He understood that the objectivity of his attempt depended on the characteristics of the window through which he would look. The fact is that we all look at what surrounds us and at ourselves through some particular window. The Cuban in question did not close off that opening which both separated and connected himself and his surroundings. Rather, he sought a kind of glass that would help him see what was most worth seeing. Instead of blocking the window, he tried to polish it, to shape its facets in such as way that it would serve as a prism to separate the important from the superfluous and magnify the essential, to make the basic colors stand out and help him undertake the kind of thinking that, being critical, allows us to break whatever spells would render the essential invisible to our gaze. As a result of this effort, Rafael Hernández (for that is his name) now presents to us *Looking at Cuba: Essays on Culture and Civil Society,* published by Letras Cubanas, containing several of his essays that first appeared between 1993 and 1999.

The title of this work gives us the key to understanding how Hernández looks at our reality: seeing Cuba *from* the viewpoint of civil society and culture. This should not surprise us. Few among us have done as much as he to disseminate this concept, not only through his essays on that topic (contained in this volume) but also through his work as editor of the magazine *Temas,* in which this idea has always been present in one form or another. But, why have recourse to that perspective? And further, what do "civil society and culture" mean? Some common definitions of both concepts, which identify civil society exclusively with nongovernmental organizations and use culture as a synonym for art, impede our understanding. Traditionally, two analytic perspectives have been privileged in the consideration of Cuban reality: one perspective from the viewpoint of the state and political space, and one from the viewpoint of the market and economic space. That privileging has limited the spectrum of topics observed and discussed: a state either strengthened or weakened, this political structure versus that one, more market or less market, a freer market or a more controlled one. Economic indices (growth rate, profitability, gross domestic product) or political indices (capacity for mobilization, membership in established organizations, power and authority, legislation and the legal framework) are rendered absolute.

What, then, is this collection of essays about? What does it mean to propose a third and alternative approach, neither political nor economic, but cultural? That puts the question badly. We must remember, above all, that no concept has been so used and debated in Cuban social science and our political scene, over the past years, as civil society. A subject does not attract that much attention unless it overlaps with power, and power is what politics and economics are about. The political dimension of the concept of civil society was made clear by the positions initially taken by two disparate groups. For those who make a profession of the counter-revolution and for the representatives of a certain liberal Catholic and non-Cuban ideology, and also for some ill-informed Cuban publicists occupying places in the ideological apparatus of the state, to adopt or reject the term "civil society" was synonymous with accepting or reject-ing the socialist ideal. So we can see that having recourse to the concept of "civil society" cannot signify, in any way, fleeing or evading questions of politics or economics. It can, however, be an alternative, a third ap-proach—not to the exclusion of the other two, but possessing a broader reach. It allows us to discuss the political and the economic from an ex-panded perspective, not as two different and separate forms of human activity, but as two interpenetrated modes of existence of the social whole. By locating the term "civil society" in the same equation as the unexpected term "culture," this author from his title on indicates to the reader, with a wink, that he is undertaking something different here. In the face of narrowly sectoral and closed analyses coming from the fields of politics and economics—which precisely because of their narrow fo-cus do not allow us to understand either the one or the other—what is proposed to us is a perspective that allows us to see our society as an organic whole. What is proposed to us is a *social* analysis. Not simply to adopt a new term, but to make use of a concept as a starting point or theoretical position from which to take responsibility for a reality—which is more complex and deeper than simply to interpret one. Such a commitment posed two challenges for the author of these texts to con-front. One was epistemological, the other political.

What was the epistemological challenge? The concept of civil society can be used with two different interpretations. There is a liberal interpre-tation, since, we should remember, this concept itself comes from liber-alism. Contemporary liberalism (though not the classic variety, which had a different understanding) has seized upon an interpretation that is highly reductionist. It sees civil society as the opposite of political society and of the state; civil society as a space reserved exclusively for free and voluntary association, the realm of the private. The state, in turn, becomes identified exclusively with the conglomeration of public institutions of repression—army, courts, executive and legislative power, et cetera—and is seen as separate from society and above it. Its function is that of gendarme. This view is congruent with a specific vision of power, one that understands power as an epiphenomenon, something that puts in an appearance after a society has taken shape; this view understands power exclusively as repression and coercion. So everything becomes clear: civil society will be on one side, the state and political society on the other. Inherent in that liberal interpretation of society is a way of thinking we may call positivist. Positivist thinking identifies and reifies. Each of its concepts is identified with a tangible, substantial and visible referent, with a *thing*. Positivism understands society as a succession of definable spaces well differentiated among themselves, laid out one alongside the next, each with its specific dynamic; these spaces hold things that themselves are easily differentiated and perceived. Thus, in the space of political society we would find things such as the state and the political parties; in that of civil society, the NGOs; in the space of the economy things like merchandise, work instruments, money. And so on, through a series of limited, demarcated, bounded spaces that contain things. Matching each space there is a branch of knowledge, a particular social science that studies only what is in front of it, without glancing to the sides at the "farms" cultivated by other social sciences alongside it. This worldview has taken root in language and common wisdom, so that any ordinary citizen is familiar with its disjunctive and dichotomous references. We speak of the relation between "state *and* society." We differentiate among the political, the economic, and the social.

Although it may seem paradoxical—at base it isn't—Marxist thinking includes an entire tradition that is dependent on liberalism and positivism, sharing their conceptual maps and epistemological patterns, if unconsciously so. When this Marxist current offers us a mechanistic and economistic version of the relationship between base and superstructure, assuring us that the base (the economy) develops first, and then the superstructure (including the state), it is reproducing the liberal interpretation of the state and power as epiphenomena. The notion of "the state of all the people" is the Stalinist translation of the liberal notion of a state situated above all classes as the arbiter of their relations. This kind of Marxism always rejected the concept of civil society, because it assumed the recent liberal version, ignoring the much more complex meaning assigned to it in the centuries of classic liberal thought from Hobbes to Hegel. This Marxism could not understand the vantage point that the concept of civil society offered for interpreting social reality, nor could it translate the idea into terms that would be useful to and consistent with a revolutionary theory. What mechanistic Marxism did understand was that the concept of civil society was alien to its anti-Marxian, state-centered interpretation of socialism.

But there is another way of taking on social reality, inspired by thinking that is truly revolutionary—consciously critical, totalizing, and opposed to reification. Its roots may be traced to the eighteenth century, but its real foundation (in the double sense of base and beginning) comes with Marx and with Gramsci. It sees society, not as a juxtaposed collection of things, but as a system of relations. It sees the state as the assemblage of structures and institutions that consolidate power. And it sees power as the structuring principle of the social whole, not only in its repressive aspect but principally in its productive one. Power is not only domination, nor even essentially domination, but hegemony: the capacity of a class to shape the cultural-spiritual atmosphere of society. And civil society is not mechanically counterposed to political society and the state, but in a relation of interpenetration with both. Civil society is the assemblage of structures and institutions that condition the socialization of the individual and the social production of meaning, which is the very function of culture. Therefore civil society is the fundamental anchor of power and the arena par excellence of political struggle.

For Rafael Hernández, the resolution of this epistemological conundrum implied a political challenge. It implied a different way of seeing the revolution and socialism—different from the way this had traditionally been done by an impoverished Marxism that is clumsily economistic and stubbornly idolatrous of the state. A conception of revolution and socialism that was not limited to the strictly political terms of taking control of the repressive public institutions, or to the strictly economic terms of achieving state ownership of the means of production, but that instead emphasized the truly political and economic terms of the socialization of power and property. A conception that understood this transformation to be a complex sociocultural process (truly political and economic) of creating a wholly new way of living and thinking, a process of constructing hegemony of a radically different sort. A conception that saw the creation of a nonalienating and liberating culture and civil society as the guarantee of this process. So, the idea of civil society would not be used as a tool to deny the validity of the socialist ideal, but would propose it in a more radical form. Marx said that to be radical was to go to the root, and that the root was man himself. To take on a perspective that stresses the concepts of hegemony and civil society means to place the human being, the production of human subjectivity, at the center of one's thought.

The urgency of this way of thinking stemmed from what we have lived through in recent years. I mean not only the processes that have occurred in the international sphere, with the collapse of self-styled "real socialism," but above all the rapid and deep changes that have occurred in Cuba. I think that is why those who presented this book in the Centro Juan Marinello on the afternoon of May 25, 2000, referred to what they called the saga of the revolutionary intellectual in the Cuba of the 1990s. The challenge imposed by these times was to think about change in the middle of change. To put forward a new viewpoint for analysis and prediction, one more radical for its humanism, in the context of rapid and profound transformations. To risk breaking with the conventional patterns and to renounce the Manichean viewpoints promoted by fundamentalists of all stripes. The work of Rafael Hernández testifies to the role played by those who set about undemonizing a theoretical approach that includes the revolutionary interpretation of civil society. These writers offered us another instrument for seeing ourselves, so that we can find a new way of constructing ourselves that will maintain continuity with the best of an ideal.

The first requirement was to think about the change going on: what it was doing to us, what its causes and meanings were. A dogmatic approach held that the change was due only to the unexpected pressure of negative external factors; therefore it was illegitimate and transitory. A critical-revolutionary Marxism, however, saw it not only as a response to the abrupt change in the international correlation of forces but above all as a necessity that grew out of the very internal processes provoked by the revolution, out of the maturation of the dynamics of change and development the revolution had unleashed. In short, as a result of the development of a new social subjectivity. The appearance of new social groups and social relations, the coming-of-age of a new generation, the accumulation of cultural changes—all of this, and more, made change necessary and therefore legitimate as well. These changes had to imply the growth of civil society and an effort to strengthen revolutionary civil society.

To insist that the issue of civil society was central to thinking about the changes going on in Cuba implied abandoning traditional, narrowly sectoral visions. It implied looking at our reality from a *social* perspective. And here we come upon an obstacle: a substantial and important part of Cuban social science—the largest part, I would say—was not prepared to do that. So it is no accident that the two articles by Hernández that opened the issue of civil society to the public should have appeared in the magazine of the Writers' and Artists' Union. I think the cause is not simply that this was one of the very few magazines to survive during those years of contraction in publishing. While others—whose professions should have obligated them to reflect on the processes under way and, still more important, to propose paths, solutions, and projects, to point out mistakes, limitations, and so on—held back, the challenge was taken up in centers like UNEAC[1] and the then Center for the Study of the Americas. They took up the task that others, whether out of intellectual incapacity or political fear, avoided. So, somewhat strangely, those who occupied center stage in this debate were artists (especially young ones) and social theory specialists not tied to traditional institutions. From the shadows where they had been relegated during the three "black five-year periods"[2] for Cuban social science, there reappeared a group of revolutionary intellectuals who up until then had been absent from the state ideological apparatus in charge of the reproduction and circulation of Marxist social thought in our schools and universities. This group had found refuge in other institutions, those that carried on theoretical-ideological debate with the outside world. Life soon showed the weakness of that artificial division (or, better, separation) within intellectual work. Wide sectors of our intellectuals, who had been put in charge of educating the new generations in a denatured Marxism, could not fulfil their appointment with history in the beginning of the 1990s. But the above-mentioned group set an example.

Taking up the point of view of civil society has several conceptual implications for the theoretical interpretation of socialism. The first is an understanding that the essential contradiction is not formulated in terms of civil society versus political society or the state, it is put forward in terms of civil society versus civil society. That is to say, there is a contradiction within civil society itself between those constitutive moments that lead toward the hegemony of international capital and those that challenge it and serve the formation of a liberatory hegemony instead. Within civil society is where the destiny of our revolution is at stake.

The second implication derives from this first one, because if the center of attention shifts to the formation of a new type of hegemony, that in turn brings to the fore the cultural dimension, in the broadest sense, of the question of power. So there is a need to renovate our conception of politics, which can no longer be understood as the construction of a passive consensus through pastoral and messianic policies. In a speech of January 13, 1996 (which has not made the impression that in my judgment it merits), Armando Hart[3] insisted on the need to develop a "cultured" politics, by which he meant one that promotes communication between diverse social sectors, democratic dialogue in the heart of the people, which develops the capacity for self-reflection and self-analysis. In full consonance with the watchword that proclaims that this revolution doesn't say to the people, "Believe!" but says to them, "Read!"[4], politics must be understood as the art of socially promoting a kind of thinking that is not only revolutionary but also autonomous, critical, and organic.

The third implication also stems from recognizing the crucial struggle within civil society between elements with opposite hegemonic signs. That implies the existence not only of internal contradictions in our society but also of antagonistic contradictions—thus breaking with simplistic formulas that presented socialism as homogeneous and harmonic. Antagonism colors the relations of popular sectors with those groups who, given a certain economic power thanks to their connections with the new patterns of accumulation, are objectively interested in promoting the free play of market forces. It also colors relations with a stand-pat bureaucracy entrenched in positions within the organs of direction and control.

On another occasion, Hart also affirmed that the great originality of the Cuban Revolution must continue to express itself in civil society. Thus he underlined an important idea. A fundamental source of our revolution was the Cuban civil society of the 1950s. The audacity of the revolution's positions, the speed and depth of its conquests, can be understood only in light of the potential contained in that civil society. Forty years later and in the midst of a crisis, history has demonstrated once again that, if Cuba survived, it was not thanks to economic riches or political agility but thanks to its "cultural capital"—whose accumulation began as far back as the eighteenth century—of which the revolution may be seen as both inheritor and promoter. The originality of the Cuban Revolution in the 1960s was expressed in the energy that, while coming from the old civil society, erupted in the formation of something new, much richer and more diverse. Previously excluded classes and social forces now appeared as political agents because they were, for the first time, cultural agents—forces for the generation and construction of new ideas, principles, ways of life, vocabulary, et cetera. Why then should there be fear of civil society? Or, more important, why should we fear the objective processes that this concept sums up?

Rafael Hernández has had the intelligence to feel uneasy, and to turn this uneasiness into action. These essays offer one proof. They do not give the reader complete solutions. Their importance lies in their capacity to incite. They incite the reader to try a different way of looking, and to confront the challenge of daring to find what one seeks.

Looking at Cuba

Notes toward a Discussion

Seeing an eye
doesn't make it an eye:
It's an eye
because it sees you.
—Antonio Machado

An old fable (Hindu or African, according to taste) tells of four blind monkeys encountering an elephant. The first describes the animal as "a flat surface, with wrinkles, and moving in and out." The second says it is "thick and cylindrical, with toenails." The third describes the elephant as "long and prehensile, with something like rings, and two panting orifices." The last submits that it is "vertical and like a rope, but with hair." Each observer is being terribly faithful to its experience of the monster. Nonetheless, the species in question remains a secret to all four.

A growing market in experiences and perceptions of Cuba—travel notes, speeches, chronicles, editorials, news articles, essays, and even books—has developed in recent times. This renewed interest, in many corners of the world, has given rise to a true eruption of "Cubanology."[1] Some of its perceptions contain curious paradoxes. In this essay I'm trying to present and discuss a brief sample of those paradoxes as seen from the Cuban perspective.

I am not unaware of the merits of the intellectual work about Cuba being done abroad, especially in academia. Emerging from a variety of ideological perspectives, this work has helped make the shortcomings of Cuban social and humanistic sciences clear to us, thus serving us as a stimulus. It has also contributed to the sum total of knowledge about Cuban problems. So the notes that follow should not be taken as an attempt to deny the intellectual value of Cuban studies outside our country. Nonetheless, many of those studies are linked to a process of ideological positioning and find their niches within a given marketplace. To that extent, they share some of the characteristics and paradoxes I am about to describe.

"To be credible, the author of a work on Cuba must be outside the country or be a 'dissident' within it."

According to this view, Cuban intellectuals lack their own perspectives and capacity for reflective thought. Either they are fainthearted or they are mere bureaucrats repeating official discourse. Dissidents, on the other hand, are a splendid species, the product of some mutation; they carry the banners of truth, integrity, and credibility. Yet if one carefully examines the list of writers about Cuba whose ideas receive the greatest distribution, one finds a peculiar logic governing this question of credibility.

For example, it may be that these authors served for many years as Cuban government officials, reaching high ranks in the civil or military bureaucracy or even in the intelligence service. Or they may simply have climbed the technocratic ladder, minding their economic p's and q's. Maybe they worked as journalists for the official media, or as experts in propaganda or censorship, or they were true believers in the Soviet outlook, or orthodox Maoists perhaps. As professors, they may have incorporated the teachings of such manuals into their academic approach. Maybe they even informed on others of their colleagues who did not seem to them ideologically hard-line enough, or they censored themselves to avoid trouble.

None of that impedes their being awarded the status of dissidents. Once they set foot on the tarmac at Gander airport, or move to Miami or Luxembourg, or declare their "dissidence," then the River Jordan has washed them clean. Overnight they become independent intellectuals with the keys to credibility in their pockets.

By way of contrast, others—whom some of the above have labeled, not without scorn, as "intellectuals"—are not treated this same way.

These others may be people who, while considering themselves revolutionaries, have faced problems because they said what they thought. For example, they may have had trouble making themselves well understood in a meeting, because some opportunist twisted their words or some extremist decided to make an example of them. Perhaps their relatives have gone north and so, since the 1960s or since the Mariel exodus, they have been living in Cuba with a considerable part of their family on the other side. Perhaps they have been labeled "conflictual" or "hypercritical" or "individualist," or even "revisionist" or "carriers of foreign influences." It's quite likely that they may know more about José Martí, Antonio Guiteras, or José Lezama Lima than the majority of those I have described above. But some book, poem, essay, or article of theirs has been questioned or censored, on account of which some of them have had to suffer ideological ostracism. Perhaps they have had to confront arrogance, sectarianism, cowardice, and the power or the weakness of others—including those others who later left or changed their stripes.

If such a person lives and works in Cuba, then he or she is viewed abroad as a functionary who is neither credible nor possessed of the ability to express his or her own ideas. A Cuban who neither leaves Cuba nor joins the organized "dissidence" is, according to established discourse of the outside, a personification of the state—a nonperson, in fact.

It is certainly true that, as Cuban intellectuals, we have not always been able to do our job without problems caused by bureaucracy, censorship, or dogmatism. But the central question here is what concrete position a given person has taken with regard to these problems, and in what political context. If self-censorship has been a way of playing according to the rules of the game set by the bureaucracy and its accomplices, it is no less true that "taking the path of freedom" has been a perfect formula for gaining access to the international marketplace.

An examination of the personal history of many paragons of credibility will demonstrate that, paradoxically, the identity card that certifies an intellectual free spirit is more available to escaped officials, repentant Stalinists, turncoat functionaries, ex-professors of dogmatism, and former straw men of cultural conformity than it is to those who always sought and fought for room to think and act on behalf of freedom, independence, and the progress of the nation, who have paid the price for this attitude without abandoning a political commitment they consciously assumed.

It is obvious that, although many accept such a Manichean view as valid, the alternative to "officialist" is not exactly "dissident." In terms of the market, though, the mutant labeled "dissident" is valued more highly than a species that has become endangered in today's world, the "revolutionary." The former, not the latter, is awarded the attribute of legitimacy.

"Fidel Castro is the source of the [Cuban] revolution and all its evils."

Recently, words like "left," "right," "conservative," and "liberal" have undergone a "semantic restructuring" or degeneration of meaning. The same has occurred with the term "dissident." Those who were always opposed, or became so very early, or were always clearly antisocialist, cannot be qualified as dissidents *strictu sensu*. Yet the long-term opposition to the Cuban Revolution has set about adopting this so-called dissidence, incorporating it to into the broad spectrum of opposition to the revolution. That opposition thus stretches, in fact, from ex-members of Acción Católica to ex-Marxists. In the midst of their irreconcilable differences, their principal shared feature may be that they are anti-Fidel.

Why is this? What is it that all of them, in common, see in Fidel? What is his role in the revolution? What is the meaning of the popular support that he enjoys?

As Theda Skocpol has pointed out, a revolution is more than the imprint of its leadership or the reflection of a revolutionary ideology. Besides being a factory that produces new politics, a revolution above all brings fundamental social transformation. Its energy is manifested in the political system and the ideological discourse, but it has its roots in civil society.

Like every true social revolution—the French, the Russian, the Chinese—the Cuban one includes several revolutions. Each social group involved in the revolutionary struggle has been able to see *its* revolution being carried out. For 150 years, after all, reformists and autonomists and annexationists and *independentistas* had been clashing in the country's ideological arena. As in other revolutions, the triumphant leadership of this one was able to defeat some of the opposing or antagonistic sectors, while joining with others that represented a much greater proportion of the social strata of the population. This was not a question simply of the effectiveness of the leaders or the solidity of the ideological propositions, but of the vast social interaction that the revolutionary politics implied.

For some, the revolution left its élan behind after the 1960s because it was no longer an adventure, a mystic experience, an epic whose objective was the destruction of the old regime and the unleashing of world revolution. Leaving aside the question of whether there were also epic moments in the '70s and '80s, I wonder: What has caused the immense majority of the population to continue supporting the revolution? Is it Marxist political thought? Liberation expeditions overseas? The Leninist party? All of these elements are part of the picture, inseparable from the process itself. But it must not be forgotten that, from the beginning, revolutionary policies and politics were supported because they signified a fundamental change in direction for the conditions of existence of the people, and a net improvement in their standard of living. During the '70s and '80s the revolutionary process achieved substantial gains in the conditions of material and cultural life of Cubans, including their social and national consciousness. This development has constituted a fundamental pillar of the revolution all these years.

If politics has to do with the art of winning internal and external support, broadening and unifying the social base, forging alliances, preserving the stability of the system, weakening opposition and foreign threats as much as possible, obtaining the respect of one's enemies, and even knowing how to achieve a certain halo of invincibility, then there are few leaders alive who have the political capacity of Fidel Castro.

Today the political leadership must run a country that does not have the kind of consensus that developed in the early '60s. It is no easy task to govern with less consensus, in the midst of discontent, among the formidable difficulties of shared scarcity, ineffective ideological communication with the outside world, and U.S. arrogance. To turn the ship in the middle of these rough seas requires appropriate ideas about democracy and economic policy. But it also requires real authority—authority that can allow for readjustment, inspire a new generation of leaders, peacefully let go of old dogmas, maintain the continuity of the revolution's essential social achievements and goals, reform the structures that were created earlier, reorder the economy and the legal system, promote more effective mechanisms, and at the same time carry out the delegation of power required for the viable transition to a more decentralized and democratic system. The one who can lead this process in the least costly manner, with the least trauma for the social body and the most stability for the country, is Fidel Castro.

This notion is not so solitary, not so unique to Cubans, as it might appear. The other side of the coin—that Fidel Castro is a factor acting contrary to the change in Cuba that hegemonic Northamerican interests hope to see—reminds Cubans that they, the *other ones,* also appreciate the importance of his role.

**"Cuban socialism consists of a political system
and an ideological discourse. Civil society has been suppressed."**

The impression given by some writings on Cuba is that Cuban society is dormant, which is to say that it hardly exists. They make it appear as if Cuban reality were made up of "the government," "the Party," and "the elite" on one side, and a passive multitude on the other. As if all the citizens capable of thought or action had moved to Hialeah or Coral Gables or had enlisted in a "human rights group." This view is worthy of discussion only because of how widespread it has become outside the island.

In the first place, the majority of Cubanologists do not generally explain what they mean by "the elite." Does this include the million members of the Party and Communist Youth? The local delegates to People's Power? Or only the list of members of the Central Committee? Or maybe only those in the Political Bureau? Does it include everyone who enjoys some kind of privilege—for instance, possession of hard currency and the opportunity to buy in special stores, as is the case for musicians, artists, athletes, or technicians who often travel abroad, or for Cubans who receive dollars from their relatives abroad? Or the members of the armed forces? Or those whose annual incomes are tens of times greater than those of a worker—as is the case for the great majority of Cuba's small private farmers, possibly the richest of Latin America? Or those who make decisions, and if so, where and about what? In the Council of State or in a corporation, in matters of religion or of agriculture?

Cuba is not the transfiguration of a doctrine, nor the reification of a totalitarian philosophy. It is a country. Little is written and even less is published about this real country, whether inside Cuba or abroad.

To do sociology about Cuban reality has not always been an option. Even now it is difficult—and more difficult still for a foreigner—to do field research. It also happens that, among those who come to Cuba to gather information, some end up collecting merely what they want to find, usually what they need to characterize the system as Stalinist or Fidel Castro as a figure down to his last days in power. Others complain that they are not given the information they need to write in a believable manner about an imperfect society. For whatever reason, the prevailing result is a sociology of images viewed from outside, which takes Havana for Cuba and takes the revolution and socialism for slogans of the moment. Such banal assumptions denature what should be profound political sociology about Cuba today.

Cuban society cannot be sociologically reconstructed as a puzzle pieced together out of political discourse. In that, it is no different from any other country in the world. Cuban society cannot be inferred from the discourse of Fidel himself, and even less so from that of his less brilliant followers. At the same time, researchers must face the fact that this discourse does continue to have a level of resonance in the population, a resonance that it would be erroneous to discount as pure emotional reaction or a mere expression of necessity.

The tendency to underestimate Cubans' level of political culture[2] is reflected in the visions predominant outside. It is also reflected, in the form of a certain paternalism, in Cuban political discourse itself. We have a broadly literate population with very high levels of access to schooling (an average of more than nine years). Cubans have known the USSR, Eastern Europe, and Africa better than any other people of the hemisphere, and, as a whole, have read more books and seen a greater variety of films than the rest of the region. They are accustomed to paying close attention to what is going on in the world, and to discussing everything from baseball to laws proposed for the approval of the National Assembly. All this poses a question: Doesn't that population have knowledge, maturity, and culture enough to face and understand the real changes that the country needs? In my opinion, it is precisely this political culture that makes the fundamental difference in Cuban society.[3] Yet our population is viewed as one with a strange incapacity to think with its head, an absurd ineptitude to decide for itself what it most needs, and a desperate need for tutelary salvation.

In other countries, reference to civil society tends to mean the middle class, the intellectuals, the entrepreneurial elite, certain influential social movements and organizations, and the like. Some of those conceptions are applied to evaluating the current situation in Cuba.

Thus, on the island, some have employed the concept of the middle layers as the "soft underbelly" of the society, identifying them with criticism and discord. Outside of Cuba, some use this same concept to define the supposed carriers of national salvation. I think that both are making the mistake of assuming that a group definable by salary levels or occupational categories possesses an ideological identity or constitutes a differentiated sociopolitical stratum.

The first, those who demonize the middle sectors as possessed by the vice of discord, are simply trying to attribute to a portion of the society a capacity for questioning that, as such, runs through the whole society. The second believe those sectors to be the medium of a part of the Cuban bourgeoisie which in the 1940s and 1950s could not take power or lacked the political courage to do so, and which in 1959 or 1960 chose the lesser of two evils as between socialism and the Northamericans; these would become the spiritual heirs of reformism.[4] Curiously, the two perceptions reveal a remarkable point of convergence.

People devoted to the arts or sciences, professionals and technicians, constitute an important group within the whole Cuban workforce, a group with an unquestionable capacity to take part in the development of the society but quite heterogeneous within itself. They may have very different tasks, display different social behavior, and naturally have different points of view. For me, they do not constitute an ideologically differentiated sector of Cuban society and so are not the possessors of an exclusive role as "critical conscience." In other words, they are not the only ones called upon, by virtue of their capacities or courage, to identify and confront the country's problems.[5] Much less are they the reservoirs of dissidence. Certainly, they are not any of these things to a greater degree than production workers, service workers, or those in other labor or educational sectors, in a country where, as Nicolás Guillén said, everything is so well mixed.

Let us take one objective indicator of social diversity: the Cubans who are leaving the country today. They don't, on the whole, reflect political dissidence, though they do reflect a degree of dissatisfaction and some very specific interests. They leave, in general, for family reasons and to gain access to a higher-level consumption market, that of the United States. Now then, who are they? Fifty percent of those who are working are production and service workers (a group that represents 65 percent of the active Cuban labor force), 36 percent are administrators (only 7 percent of the work force), and just 13 percent of the employed persons leaving are professionals and technicians (though the representation of this group in the Cuban workforce is a good deal higher, at 21 percent). The proportion of high-professional-level emigrants is much lower today than it was in the '60s and '70s. In a more homogeneous society, as Cuba is in the '90s, there are more direct production or service workers migrating than there were in those earlier years. The immense majority of those who leave do represent the higher overall level of education in Cuba; however, naturally, they are not university graduates but people who have finished primary or secondary school.[6]

Paradoxically—and this is perhaps the paradox par excellence of Cuban socialist society—criticism, disagreement, and even demands are nothing if not the children of the revolution itself at the level of civil society. Cubans truly consider themselves equal citizens, and not only in the text of the Constitution of the Republic. In other words, any Cuban, whether a black resident of Old Havana, a peasant in the Escambray, a youth walking in any city park or seafront, a retired person living in any apartment building, or a working mother who is head of her household—all these Cubans consider themselves capable of asserting this right, out loud, accompanied by a declaration of complaints about what the system, and especially the state, owes them as rightful members of civil society.

The question is: Should we regret having created these demanding citizens who, accustomed as they are to the munificence or even paternalism of the socialist state, think they deserve an adequate level of health and education services, social security, work opportunities, and so forth, in the midst of the current crisis? Or, on the contrary, should we congratulate ourselves on this level of political culture and social consciousness engendered by the revolution, which is pressuring the socialist leadership today? This social phenomenon would pose serious difficulties for any project of "pure socialism" and isolation from the world at all costs. It would also pose serious difficulties for the return of capitalism to Cuba. Such an imposition would run the risk of unleashing great social tensions.

Indeed, what would be the reaction of these Cubans who, unlike the poor of Latin America and other regions, have become accustomed during more than thirty years to being *inside* rather than *outside*? What would they say if they were informed that the achievements of socialism have been the result of a mistake, of an historical aberration, and that the truth of the modern world is that their portion is almost nil? On the other hand, the majority of Cubans do not want to live egalitarianly poor. Workers in general legitimately aspire to salary compensation that reflects a level of access to the market. In terms of equal opportunity as well as in other dimensions of the new model, it would be tragic to renounce the main thrust of social justice, solidarity, independence, and freedom that makes up the nucleus of Cuban revolutionary ideas—and that is nothing but the natural fruit of Cuba's own history.

"Cuba is the same as ever. It is just going through a process of surface or temporary changes."

For some, the revolution is an aberration, a monster of the dream of reason, so to speak. In fact, however, since the nineteenth century Cuba has rarely gone through three decades without a crisis of economic, political, and social change. These periodic crises have been characterized by strong ideas about renewal, progress, development, social justice, national vindication, and independence. The Marxist socialist outlook flowed naturally into this historical channel.

The difficulties of the current crisis often hide that long-term dynamic's stubborn consistency. Some outside observers seem to be discussing a present with no history, as if the future could be predicted after the manner of those ancient cosmographies described by Borges, in which the world was still new. On our shores, some *compañeros* believe that the revolutionary leadership has a demiurgical power to shape social reality according to its desires. Both groups forget that we are not in

1959. They underestimate the real political force of the Cuban people, the product of historical accumulation and—as discussed above—a unique political culture.

Popular support for the system is what gives it stability. Continued identification of the system with the interests of the population guarantees it support. In spite of the relative erosion of consensus in the last few years, what is most notable is how much that equilibrium has been maintained.

In fact, the system has now demonstrated an exceptional capacity for assimilation. Could such a brutal drop in levels of economic growth have been cushioned to a comparable degree in any other country of Latin America? To be sure, it's not much consolation for Cuba's population, confronting the overload of daily life, to know that Latin America has 200 million poor. Nor would it be prudent to conclude that their capacity for endurance is invulnerable or unlimited. People do not confront the hard things of life in peacetime the same way they do under the bombs, nor do governments command the same political resources or instruments of power.

The Cuban people's endurance is matched by an expectation of change. The debate preceding the Fourth Party Congress—the deepest and widest process of critical analysis that Cuba's socialist society has known—resolved itself in favor of decentralization, economic efficiency, more popular participation in decision making, democratization of the country's political institutions (starting with the Communist Party itself and the National Assembly), effective means of political representation (especially elections), and an end to discrimination against religious believers and other sectors such as youth, women, and blacks.

Objectively, to the extent that economic difficulties and external pressures affect the space for internal debate, limit the decentralization process, and contribute to maintaining the stress on defense, they do not favor the process of change. Democratic styles don't find a friendly climate in fortresses under siege.

However, that does not mean that solving the problems of the political system can be de-emphasized or postponed. Though the major effort is dedicated to the difficult task of supplying food and articles of primary need, this does not imply that the necessary restructuring of institutions and rectification of the system can be dropped. Survival tactics will not get very far without a political and economic development strategy suited to the new conditions reigning in the world. Classically, while the economy may seem to be determinant, politics really is.

The process of political reforms does not have to be based on certificates of good conduct issued by "international" institutions like the Carter Center at Emory University or America's Watch, a U.S.-based organization that monitors human rights violations in Latin America. Neither do the decentralization of the economic system, the opening of a space for certain forms of Cuban private initiative, and collaboration with foreign capital imply the implementation of neoliberal-style reforms that wipe out the state's role in the economy.

Indeed, the July 1992 reform of the Cuban Constitution has opened the legal possibility of redefining the nature of property, including its private use in the case of "nonfundamental means of production," and of modifying the irreversible character of the socialist sector, as well as recognizing the form of property represented by foreign investments.[7] Similarly, while allowing private investments and a less administrative concept of state planning, the constitutional reform gave more autonomy to state enterprises themselves, which could point toward a system with both planning and more freedom in mercantile relations.[8]

In the terrain of politics and ideology, the majority of the constitutional reforms tended to redefine the context for greater pluralism. First, the bases of the state were defined in terms of "people" and "workers," rather than a particular social class or stratum.[9] Second, the laic character of the Cuban state was announced, explicitly proscribing any form of religious discrimination, thus excluding atheism as the official ideology.[10] Third, the system of People's Power was broadly reformed, establishing (among other important changes) direct popular election of the National Assembly and the provincial assemblies, and fundamentally modifying the municipal and provincial administrative apparatus.[11]

Finally, the reformed constitution presents the Party not as the vanguard of one particular class but of the Cuban nation.[12] That implies a differentiation between political pluralism and a multiparty system. The fact is that none of the fundamental problems of today's Cuba would be automatically resolved by having multiple parties. But the Cuban Communist Party does now face a challenge. One of the main hurdles it faces in the coming years is to really make itself the party of the Cuban nation, to welcome various currents of thought that reflect the feelings of the people, without thus losing its strength, unity, and capacity to direct the country's development and the preservation of its independence and national sovereignty.

Might Cuba need more than one party in the future? I think that, independently of the preferences of Cuban revolutionary stalwarts, the answer would objectively depend on their capacity to face the challenge just mentioned. Of course, the political unity represented by the Party remains an unquestionable strategic necessity in the face of the constant threat that the United States poses to the sovereignty of the country. What would happen if this threat ended or were substantially reduced? In any case, a future and more democratic Cuba would not resemble the Cuba of the 1950s. It would be a Cuba that, while popular and pluralist, would not allow annexationist or autonomist parties, or representatives of entrepreneurial interests—a system where politics would not become an electoral or parliamentary exercise far removed from the interests and needs of the population, much less a proliferation of special interests with money from Miami or Washington which could fragment and block the state actions needed to protect the overall interests of the country.

The real issue of democracy in Cuba—not in the abstract, according to definitions in vogue in countries whose citizens barely vote—is the capacity of the population to self-govern (in lowercase) and exercise control over the Government (uppercase). It is not only about self-government and control in the *act* of electing, but especially in the *process* of governing. If democracy is conceived as part of a social process in motion, not merely as a formula allowing parties to rotate the possession of power, then in meeting that challenge Cuban society—with all its failings— would have advanced further down the long and difficult path to democracy than any other society in this hemisphere.

Postscript

The chorus of foreign attitudes toward the Cuban situation that I've tried to describe (without ill humor, I hope) hides a diversity of motives. The majority of the members of that chorus see Cuba through a filter of received truths, commonplaces, and simplifications; they are the friends of black-and-white. Then there is a familiar group of enemies, those who always knew that socialism here was evil and now console themselves with the idea that it is coming to an end. Finally, there are those who once called themselves socialists and later renounced this mirage. They neither repeat set phrases nor rub their hands in expectation; rather, they await the end of socialism as a necessary part of their second thoughts. They watch the collapse with a certain bitterness, but at the same time they feel the relief of finding evidence that they did not make a mistake, while they gravely nod their heads at the stubborn reality in which the dreams of men explode.

In Cuba, those who believe in—as Fidel would say—miracle formulas,[13] whether monetary mechanisms or foreign investment, reflect a peculiar pragmatism expressed in the idea of a change under duress toward who knows what. Those pragmatists are the other side of the coin of the inveterate ideologues: both lack new, clear, and distinct ideas about the possible future to which they aspire. The question is, How are current changes tied to that future? Above all, how can we rethink the system so that the future—as Martí would say—is not simply one in which the strongest prevail?

3

Civil Society and Its Surroundings

In *Utopia Unarmed*—a title that history placed in doubt almost immediately after it appeared—Mexican political scientist Jorge G. Castañeda judges the Latin American left for placing excessive hopes on civil society. Castañeda's text serves an example of the misunderstandings and polemics spawned by the genealogy and, especially, the current use of this term. Here in Cuba, too, the concept has given rise to various sorts of interpretations and implications, as is reflected in the thorough commentary by my colleague Armando Cristóbal.[1]

Since I believe I am in agreement with the main part of his comments and especially with their spirit, I would prefer to use the opportunity presented by his letter to return to a topic whose importance, I think, cannot be overestimated.

The issue of civil society brings multiple problems in its wake. The term refers to phenomena that emerged in social movements, grassroots organizations, and the so-called nongovernmental organizations within such varying contexts as Europe and Latin America. At the same time, it is a concept employed in a controversial and not always clearly defined manner in political analysis—for example, some see it as a part of bourgeois discourse, lacking in any usefulness to Marxism. Finally, it tends to be appropriated for various ideological uses that often have very little to do with its strict definition.

Some authors identify it with an originally Hegelian concept, which established the dichotomy of state versus civil society.[2] They explain its popularity in Latin America as a reaction against traditional Marxism, to which they attribute the error of having assumed that only the state had any importance as a political institution. They identify Gramsci's contribution as a return to Hegel, whose merit thus would reside in his having produced a more holistic appreciation of political activity. In civil society they find the nuclei of resistance and, in general, the engines of political change in Eastern Europe.[3] And they see it represented by the popular movements—human rights committees, religious communities, indigenous people's organizations—that have proliferated in Latin America in the past decade.

As may be guessed, the subject is not so purely philosophical as it may at first appear. Typically, it belongs to a theoretical field which gives rise to considerations and evaluations of concrete facets of politics. But there is an eminently conceptual dimension that we must consider first.

The Classic Explanations

The term "civil society" has, historically, had quite varied uses and abuses. Hobbes and Locke, the fathers of Anglo-Saxon natural law, used it long before Hegel and Marx to designate the society that had ceased to be primitive and organized itself around the principles of a commonly accepted political power. In the Enlightenment, on the other hand, Rousseau postulated that merely civil(ized) society was historically insufficient to be a fully human form of organization, and that this fullness could be realized only with the coming of "political society," or the state.

More than a space structurally opposed to the state, Hegelian civil society is a step toward it. For Hegel, civil society grows out of the disintegration of a purely familial social organization, which makes room for the rise of classes and of elements of the state, although the state still has not reached its full-blown form. The uniqueness of the state lies in its capacity to place itself "above" the particular interests of classes. However, it would be an exaggeration to say that Hegel placed the state completely "outside" civil society, given that he himself said that state regulations were an integral part of civil society. That is, the Hegelian concept already acknowledges a mutual interaction between state and civil society—a nuance of central importance for modern political theory.

Marx would later say that, in studying Hegel, he had reached the conclusion that political and legal institutions had their roots in the material conditions of life, whose totality Hegel grouped under the name of civil society, and that it was necessary to seek the anatomy of civil society in political economy. As is well known, Marx did not employ the concept the same way as Hegel, nor did he use it only in his "youthful" works, as the above paraphrase, taken from the "Prologue," will attest.[4] Some observers conclude that for Marx (and for later political theory) civil society was nothing more than the natural society of Hobbes and Locke, or the blind order of natural and economic relationships, from which stemmed the need to progress to political society or the state. Or, to put it more simply, that civil society represents the sphere of the private, while the state embodies the public sphere.[5]

In my judgment, in Marx himself this approach does not appear in such a schematic way. It is true that at times, when presenting his viewpoint in a simplified fashion, he reduces the concept of civil society to "the form of interchange corresponding to [the bourgeois] mode of production and created by it."[6] But at other times he is quite a bit more nuanced: "To given phases of the development of production, commerce, and consumption there correspond given forms of social constitution, a *given form of family organization, of estates or of classes; in a word, a given civil society.* To a given civil society there corresponds a given political state, which is nothing more than the official expression of civil society" [italics mine].[7]

This paragraph offers several eloquent clues.

First, it makes clear that for Marx—as for Armando Cristóbal and myself—civil society does not equal the overall society or its socioeconomic form, which strictly speaking would include the superstructure as well.

Second, if indeed Marxists affirm that "the will of the state obeys, in general, the variable needs of civil society," referring to civil society above all as the "realm of economic relations,"[8] this does not mean that it is reduced to the merely "economic" plane of the social structure.

Finally, it is evident that Marx is not reproducing Hegel, but is locating the concept in a new theoretical context, clearly distinguishing the relationship and the limits of civil society and the state. This new approach shows what is new in the Marxist conception because, as distinct from his predecessors (Hegel included), Marx's theory is oriented precisely toward demonstrating the historical validity of a society that can function without a state. The communist model represents precisely the emancipation of the individual upon his or her joining, in communitarian fashion, in a society where the state, in its role of domination, would have withered away.

Gramsci uses the concept in various senses, but always relates it to the themes of hegemony and domination.[9] In general, he uses it to refer to the sphere of ideological-cultural relationships which represent the consensus. In one of his most frequently used senses, the state is the apparatus of coercion, while the institutions through which hegemony is exercised—schools, mass media, other cultural institutions—constitute civil society. Far from considering this a simple antagonism, the Gramscian vision highlights the correspondence, even the functional relationship, between civil society and state. Contrary to the readings that Castañeda and others have given him, Gramsci does not use the concept in a Hegelian sense.

In the sense in which it most commonly appears in contemporary literature, civil society is the sphere of relations among individuals, groups, and social classes outside the institutional power relationships characteristic of the state. Northamerican schools of thought tend to use it as a synonym for society,[10] giving society the connotation of a subsystem, along with other subsystems such as politics and economics. But in European schools, civil society is used along lines that have followed Marx—as a term in the same equation as the state, each varying according to the variation of the other.

Naturally, prophets of the rupture of an established order also have recourse to the term civil society to talk about a return to a previous or primary order which they see as more just. But there are also critics of this supposed order who warn that civil society cannot be reduced to a barrier for the containment of government excesses, as liberalism would have it, because it too includes institutions that limit individual freedom. Corporate associations and other powerful groups, communications media and bureaucratic structures all act as conditioners of the conduct of the social subject in contemporary capitalist society, thus limiting democratic participation.[11]

A minimal analysis of fundamental theoretical sources[12] allows us to determine the following:

(a) The issue of the relation between civil society and state cannot be reduced to a Hegelian approach nor to the currents that identify the two terms as polar opposites, mutually exclusive, or antagonistic.

(b) The difference between civil society and political society is a matter discussed both before and after Marx. The Marxist contribution consists of having defined a particular relationship between the two, which Marx was the first to recognize and which has been enriched by later Marxist thinking.

(c) Neither Marx nor later Marxist thinking has seen civil society as "the sphere of the nonpolitical" or the "nonideological," much less as lacking in political importance. Rather, they see it as the field in which the forces that transform or affect political power arise.

(d) Civil society is seen today essentially as the sphere of tensions and conflicts which are then brought to the state. In this sense, the state has an interest and a responsibility to seek new sources of legitimization and areas of consensus in civil society.

Civil Society in Socialism

Although civil society is a concept long incorporated into Marxist discourse, the right has recently become enamored of it.[13] A kind of distortion characteristic of the discourse about contemporary Cuban civil society is expressed in the abuse of this concept, especially by writers who study Cuba from afar. They paint state and civil society as paired in a mutually exclusive antagonism in spite of the fact that, as we have just seen, this reductionism has little to do with the majority of recognizable uses of the concept in theoretical work.

What has come into vogue is the ideological use of the term civil society constructed as a scene of destabilization of the system. This verbal operation attempts to issue new identity cards to highly political actors, as if they were spontaneous expressions of an ideologically neuter society. When I refer to certain paradoxical perceptions that predominate outside Cuba,[14] I'm pointing specifically to ideas like those that define

Cuban civil society as springing from unlikely sources including the right-wing Cuban-American organizations based in Miami.[15]

The only reason to call attention to such an obvious manipulation is that, like other traps, sometimes it works in reverse. Thus, some *compañeros* in Cuba represent civil society as the realm of conservatism and society's regressive forces. They even react to this trick by arguing, so to say, that "the enemy wants to implant civil society here." This is a poor defense against an ideological operation that attempts to appropriate established language and recognizedly progressive ideas like "democracy," "human rights," or "pluralism." That reaction to the ideological *use* of the term "civil society" suffers from intellectual inconsistency and, being limited to a defensive position, is also ideologically ineffective.

Recognizing the traits that distinguish the state from civil society does not require us to see them as factors in irreconcilable conflict. In fact, in "Looking at Cuba" I have taken a position in opposition to the polar division of state and civil society. I believe that socialism does not manifest itself only in a political system and an ideological discourse, nor can it develop organically if it does not have roots in civil society,[16] as became obvious in the tragic case of Eastern Europe. In Cuba the revolution was not a change of regime or the rise of a communist party to government power, but a fundamental social transformation; it was and continues to be a process with deep social roots, as characterized by Marx and as can be found in the Cuban revolutionary tradition—not in that of "some currents of thought" today. In fact, this idea of revolution is implanted in Cuban political culture from José Martí to Fidel Castro. The concept of a people as a social subject, for instance, also belongs to this culture, right along with the set of problems defined by civil society.[17]

In Cuba, revolutionary power transformed civil society and the state, opening new spaces of political action. But socialism has meant a system of organization of the whole society, not only the state or the political system. Socialist civil society has grown more and more complex and heterogeneous since the 1960s.[18] That is why, when basic changes are proposed and made in the economy, they will in all probability give rise to changes in social structure, in relations between social classes and strata, which must be balanced by corresponding adjustments in the political sphere. The continuity of revolutionary society requires changes in the political system to follow a logic of social development, so that the state can compensate for inequalities and other negative factors arising in civil society. To achieve that end requires an effective process of interaction with the needs and interests of the social bases of the system, which implies a greater participation of the citizenry in decision making and in control of the political process.

Without a consensus within civil society, not only will the legitimacy of revolutionary power be affected, but so will the stability and continuity of the system itself. If the ideological-cultural dimension[19] does not receive sufficient attention, if a holistic perspective on the sphere of economic organization or on the order of social and class relations is lost, the revolutionary process itself could be harmed. All of these are specifically defined as being within the terrain of civil society.

The foregoing indicates the necessity and usefulness of recovering this concept for the purpose of examining Cuba's problems. An emphasis on our civil society emphasizes, above all, an integrated sociological perspective on political and ideological phenomena as seen from the point of view of social relations. This perspective is even more necessary when the dynamic of civil society has become blurred by the high degree of politicization of social relations and social institutions in Cuba. We need an approach that restores the specificity and autonomy of the *social* as a factor that interacts with the *institutionally political*. And carrying out such an analysis—as Cristóbal also correctly points out in his commentary—requires diligent study of concrete problems. That is, it requires the social sciences (and every field of social research and practice) to contribute to adequately clarifying and delineating the groups, institutions, and emerging messages of civil society—even if what is diagnosed does not always meet our desires and expectations.

Civil Society and Political Culture

The problems confronting Cuban socialist society are broader than what economic analysis can reveal, because the causes and consequences of the crisis extend beyond this one dimension.[20] But even within this narrow frame, it is obvious that in Cuba the "realm of economic relations" has changed in recent years. This is true not only because of the reorientation of international trade and financing or relations with foreign capital. The functioning of the economic "realm" in current conditions—that is, the process of civil society in this period of restructuring—includes phenomena ranging from the informal economy (marked by a growth in self-employment and in the black market)[21] to the emergence of a new stratum of labor attached to the joint-venture sector of the economy (with characteristics strongly different from the rest).

The set of problems stemming from these transformations is a fundamental one. What is the impact of the economic changes already implemented, and those now approaching, on the social structure and class and strata relations in Cuban civil society? How does the rapid modification of the relationship among work, income, and access to consumption affect different social groups, from workers to the marginalized, in the context of the maintenance of an egalitarian and redistributive social policy and, at the same time, the growth of the underground economy? How do peasants and workers, administrators and intellectuals, youth and housewives all experience this process in differentiated ways?

Since the debate spurred by the Call to the Fourth Party Congress in 1990—updated to some degree by the recent trade-union-organized discussion of the most pressing economic measures in the first third of 1994—the heartbeat of Cuban public opinion about a variety of national problems has been heard. This civil society is definitely not mute.[22] The differing projections of distinct social sectors in the spaces for political participation are significant in developing an understanding of the dynamic of civil society in Cuban socialism.

For example, according to a recent study, intellectuals (professionals and technicians) in today's Cuba are characterized by an accentuated predisposition toward criticism, combined with a comparatively high index of political commitment.[23] This sector has a relatively developed self-perception regarding its social mission; at the same time, it tends to a more integrated reflection about the overall problems of the system, accompanied by worries about the factors that affect the political project.[24] Logically, the intellectuals tend to place a special value on that critical function, perhaps more so than other sectors, but in any case consistent with the values of the revolutionary political culture.

Those traits identified in the attitudes of professionals and technicians (and other traits equally deserving of discussion) are, however, not essentially different from the ways that members of other social sectors, at their grassroots levels, relate to the state institutions and to the system in general.

This is the case, for instance, with churches and religious associations. Some authors consider them the preeminent "subversive" organizations in Cuban civil society.[25] If we take into account that popular religious feeling in Cuba is not precisely Catholic, that logic would identify the *casas templos* of the Regla de Ocha or Palo Monte (the homes in which the practices of these Afro-Cuban religions take place) as reservoirs of opposition. Yet even studies done outside Cuba, which question the socialist system, recognize that "the majority of *santeros* support the Revolution." Among the evangelical churches there is also noteworthy political activism in solidarity with the Cuban government's social policies. And, in general, it must be recognized that the prospects for Cuban religious associations are better now than at any other time since 1959.[26] These facts illustrate the complex and interactive relationship between state and civil society in Cuba.

For some, the concept of civil society is limited to describing the "human rights groups" or "dissident organizations." Those groups unite and subdivide in such a manner that it is difficult to refer to them as a defined sector, much less discover their connection with sectors of Cuban civil society. Their chief common trait appears to be the contrast between their notoriety abroad and their lack of real presence in Cuban civil society itself.[27] Apart from "being against," their agendas do not reveal much ideological identity or organic relation to specific social components of civil society.

A systematic analysis of Cuban civil society would require more space and empirical referents than I can include in these comments, which are limited to putting forward a general overview of the subject. For example, it would require deeper examination of the participation in Cuban social dynamics and politics of specific social groups or classes, such as youth or peasants, and of the role played by the base-level membership of Cuban organizations. An exhaustive analysis of the process of transformation the country is going through would also require more consideration of the way that state institutions, the government, and the political leadership in general are involved in those changes.

By way of ending, I would like to at least mention two other basic problems, intimately connected with each other and with the subject of civil society: the issue of political culture, and that of participation.

All conceptual and practical thinking about political culture assumes the critical significance of civil society. Unlike ideology, political culture (as an interconnected system of political knowledge and values and actual conduct) is formed in a socialization process that goes beyond the inculcation of values and the political institutions and apparatus. What determines the political culture of individuals is the family, the media, the schools, youth organizations, religious and social organizations, and, in general, the sites where those individuals themselves participate.[28] As Richard Fagen pointed out years ago about Cuba, a change in political culture cannot be isolated from citizen participation or from institutional change.[29]

In today's Cuba, the spaces for the participation of civil society in the articulation of the political system—cultural spaces included—constitute organic segments of the socialist system which must be broadened and strengthened. This civil society is the foundation of socialism in Cuba, which means the origin of its institutional system as well. Recognizing civil society, responding to it, preserving it, interacting with it—these are all strategic for the policies of the revolution.

4

The Second Death of Dogma

Notes on a Culture of the Left

> The importance of our struggle lies in
> the fact that it is antidogmatic.
> —Subcomandante Marcos, EZLN

When the Zapatista Army of National Liberation (EZLN) broke down the doors of the town hall of San Cristóbal de Las Casas on January 1, 1994, it simultaneously dethroned the theory that a Latin American popular rebellion could arise and develop only if it had the direct support of Cuba.

That thesis, formulated like one of those immutable laws in certain manuals of Marxism, had previously gone like this: "Given the conditions for revolution in a Latin American country, it will not develop without the spark of Cuban intervention. If the Cuban factor is present but the necessary conditions are not, the revolution will not develop either. Only with the conditions and Cuban aid will an armed struggle successfully develop and advance."[1] Like the rule of three.

Since the era in which the so-called guerrilla *foco* theory attempted to translate the rich and complex experience of the Cuban Revolution into a discourse on revolutionary method, there have been many attempts to extract general laws about the functioning of political movements or social conflicts in the region. With greater or lesser success, these writers have tried to capture the essence of a knotty subject characterized by a scattered informational base, questionable oral sources, strong political bias in almost all available assessments, and monumental differences among the national experiences under study. In *Utopia Unarmed*, Jorge Castañeda has taken up this formidable challenge.

Written at times like a magic-realist thriller (we Latin Americans do have a tendency toward what Alejo Carpentier called the "marvelous real") and at times with the tidy symmetry of a Harvard doctoral dissertation, Castañeda's book stimulates reflection on the culture of the left in Latin America. If we keep in mind that the "political culture of the left" is diverse and contradictory, perhaps an assemblage of subcultures, and that *Utopia Unarmed* represents a particular approach to it, then we could say that my comments fit within that larger area of reflection. I will try, in the first place, to discuss Castañeda's basic theses about the role of intellectuals in Latin America, which are contained in the chapter of his book currently available to Cuban readers. In the second place, starting from that Latin American frame of reference—and from the implications, lessons, and faults of the chapter in question—I will attempt a critical reflection on the intellectual movement in Cuba, its relation to politics and, of course, its relation to problems of culture.

Does Latin America Follow Rules? Three Theorems

To explain the role of intellectuals in Latin American societies and politics over the past decade, Castañeda begins with a peculiar sociological premise: he takes as his interpretive hypotheses what these intellectuals think about themselves. That leads him to three general theorems drawn from, respectively, Carlos Fuentes, Carlos Monsiváis, and Gabriel García Márquez:

(1) Intellectuals have fulfilled a crucial and disproportionate function in the societies and politics of Latin America.

(2) At the end of the 1960s and the beginning of the 1970s, the intellectual left acquired a mass base for the first time.

(3) There is a special relationship between intellectuals and political power in Latin America, to the point where, in the history of power, there are only military dictatorships and intellectuals.

These theorems, I believe, are all based on a certain conception of Latin American civil society. Compared with more developed Western societies, this outlook would have it, our societies are unstructured, they can barely sustain nations that have never managed to complete themselves, and they subsist in a fashion disconnected from the rest of the world. In sum, they might be called subsocieties.

From this premise spring twin ideas. The first is that Latin American intellectuals have historically replaced civil society, supplanted its groups and "living forces," and become the mouthpieces of movements that otherwise had only a larval sort of existence. To put it in terms not much used today, the intellectuals became the inorganic expression of sectors and classes that lacked a consciousness of themselves.

The second idea is that a swarm of previously unknown social movements are now arising from this amorphous civil society, as products of the exhaustion of the old parties and model of accumulation, and also thanks to other aspects of the endless decade of the '80s, including the end of the dictatorships. Further, the left confuses these movements with the "road to revolution." Latin America's weak civil society, which according to Castañeda the intellectuals had been defending against the authoritarian state since colonial times, has finally come of age and occupied the space that the intellectuals previously needed to hold as its proxy. According to this interpretation, the Latin American left has been dazzled yet again, this time succumbing to the "ideological spell" of a popular movement that at last exists outside of university classrooms and party meetings.

In this vision of the labyrinths of Latin American history, intellectuals continue to be important social actors, but the new circumstances have altered the centuries-old role they had felt obligated to assume. Surprising as it may seem, this radical transformation in a five-hundred-year-old historical pattern occurred in the 1980s—in front of our own eyes, so to speak—without the majority of us taking note.

In my judgment, that logic reflects a conceptual confusion about the relations between state and civil society.[2] It also transplants a Eurocentric model to Latin American civil society. Similar transplants based on European or Northamerican models attempt (if without great effort) to demonstrate that we do not have parties, social classes, capitalism, or socialism, because these do not appear in the same form as in other countries where everything is supposedly clear and distinct.[3]

Furthermore, this vision presupposes a Latin American civil society that the omnipotent states of the region can systematically annul. Let us examine to what degree this is so.

In the cases of the power exercised by bureaucratic-authoritarian states[4], what prevails is coercive domination of civil society, rather than hegemony over it. Domination is based on coercion, while hegemony has more to do with consent. In Latin America, historically, states have governed more through compulsion than through consent. To a great extent, the raison d'être of the authoritarian state reflects its incapacity to hegemonically coopt civil society. As a result, effective and stable control tends to be less deeply implanted in the social substratum.

Castañeda's view implies that in European countries or the United States, areas of the globe where civil society is supposedly stronger, the state must be weaker. Are we to conclude that the social control exercised by the Western democracies is less effective? No, I would argue, because that control is not based so much on coercive domination as on hegemony over civil society as a whole, where the state penetrates through ideological-cultural mechanisms to a much greater degree than in our lands.

Finally, Castañeda's perception postulates that the emergence or leading role of civil society in Latin America is a recent or unprecedented phenomenon. But civil society does not appear to have been silenced, excluded from history, or annulled in Bolivia, Colombia, or even in Central America, Cuba, or Mexico itself, although at times, yes, it has been weakened. In many of these countries, peasant, self-defense, or labor movements have historically been strong, which explains outbreaks of social unrest and revolutions. That those movements have sometimes fallen into the spheres of influence of political parties or been coopted by state institutions does not mean that they don't exist, or that they exist to a lesser degree than in industrialized countries. Do environmentalists or gays in Germany or the United States float in some social space isolated from all power, from political and ideological currents, or even from electoral campaigns?

In truth, we have to ask whether the rise of civil society in the '80s results from a weakening of the Latin American state or instead from the resurgence and renewal of social movements, some of them as old as the indigenous communities, as well as the efforts of powerful social groups to develop hegemonic mechanisms to replace the less-and-less-profitable coercion of the dictatorships. Might the political parties not be so weak, nor the repressive apparatus so diminished—since, below the surface of the democracies, it remains intact—but rather might they both show a tendency to carry out their roles of social control less and less effectively?

A deeper examination would identify the actors from below as expressions of a social insurgency that is not necessarily "armed," in the strictly military sense preferred by Castañeda, nor exactly "unarmed" in the sense of lacking access to alternative means of power. At the same time, it would note that this process takes place in a new domestic and international context where the dominant classes (if I may use that term) require a strategic reaccommodation in accord with new patterns of production and modes of accumulation. This new situation requires them to seek a new blueprint for the rebuilding of consensus, one that leaves out a reasonable portion of the population but gives a certain space to another portion, represented in a variety of sectors of civil society. The contemporary rise in Latin America of issues such as democracy is closely connected to both phenomena: social insurgency and the redesigning of consensus.

All of this leads us, finally, to the question of the intellectuals. For Castañeda and his authors of choice, intellectuals are a variety of Latin American knight errants who have managed to convert themselves into the generators of the antidictatorial resistance movements. Yet this does not seem to really be the case in, say, Central America, where the popular sectors and the political leadership of the revolutionary left have struck the strongest blows against the power of a state based on the armed forces and oligarchies.

In the majority of countries of the Latin American region, the democratic spaces carved out in the '80s appear not to have resulted from the separate action of the intellectuals, many of whom were in exile, but instead from the political parties and popular movements inside the countries, which made it harder for the dictatorships to govern. Without underestimating the importance of intellectuals in this process, it would be an exaggeration to claim, as Castañeda's theory does, that the process took place thanks to ideologies that the intellectuals imported in the '70s and '80s—that the intellectuals served as a vehicle for international influences that determined change.

The theorems in *Utopia Unarmed* suffer from a certain ontologism. They reflect the idea that the Latin American phenomena under discussion are new, resembling nothing in human history, and will never be seen again. But the fact that the state in Latin America tries to establish a relationship with intellectuals that will serve its interests, and that there are powerful groups who would prefer to have the intellectuals on their side, represents neither a specifically Latin American trait nor anything new in the history of political power. The state's attempts to seduce and use the intellectuals are as old as the classical civilizations of Greece and Rome. This phenomenon has not occurred everywhere or at all times, but in no way is it something unique to the novelists of the Latin American 1960s "boom."

There have been periods of alliance between the intellectuals and the popular bases before in our region, and there have been periods of distance as well. Since the time of the independence movements, intellectuals' political participation and popular projection have generally surged in the periods of ideological confrontation preceding revolutionary outbreaks, including the student movements of the 1920s and the 1960s to which Castañeda points. One such period was, precisely, the years of the insurgencies of the 1960s, with their guerrilla groups, student rebellions, and other popular opposition movements. In that era, intellectuals exercised an undeniable influence from the lecterns of the universities and the columns of the press. Still, it would be very hard to support a claim that they acted primarily as a separate group or as individuals—as autonomous entities without links to movements, vanguards, or political elites. Organically or not, their role merged and merges with a political dynamic in which diverse actors participate. That they may appear onstage more often than others does not make them the absolute protagonists. Especially if we consider that, as José Martí said—and the Mexican author of *Utopia Unarmed* knows this full well—in politics, what's real is what's unseen.[5]

Finally, the political phenomenology of the contemporary world is a good deal more complex than a dichotomy whereby Latin American intellectuals involuntarily accept a role that does not really belong to them. If it is true that they have participated in politics to an important degree, still it would be hard to show that the sometime public servants Fernando Henrique Cardoso or Octavio Paz played roles essentially different from those of André Malraux or Arthur Schlesinger Jr. It is possible, perhaps, to see Latin American intellectuals as being more multifaceted than those of other latitudes—in the same way that our philosophers are less purely philosophers, and their philosophy tends to have a more eclectic stamp than is found in, say, the Germanic tradition.[6] But this is not because, as Carlos Alberto Montaner has declared, we Latin Americans lack the Europeans' sense of intellectual discipline and selfless devotion. Rather, it is because our culture, and therefore its expression in our social relations and politics, is different.

Naturally, the politicization of the cultural agenda tends to be more or less charged according to the historical period. During the 1960s, for example, intellectual debate grew highly politicized throughout the world. This was part of a more general effect created by the convulsions of the period as they were spread by the new communications technologies. These technologies—outside the power of the intellectuals—projected a new global political culture beyond strictly intellectual media. More recently, the ideological dislocation resulting from the end of the Cold War and certain readings of postmodernity have characterized a period in which the theme of political commitment does not figure so much in cultural debate, although I would not say that the political vocation of intellectuals has declined so much.

In any case, this phenomenon of politicization goes beyond the question of the role of intellectuals and becomes entwined with other contemporary themes that affect the culture of the left. In this, as in other aspects, the case of Cuba is less exceptional than is often assumed.

The Image of Cuba

For many Latin American intellectuals, the Cuban Revolution represented the dream of emancipation, the utopia of freedom achieved. It also meant access to the world market for culture. In the 1960s, Cuba put Latin America in fashion. Many of the writers of the literary boom, the new cinema, and sociological dependency theory were (and in numerous cases still are) supporters of Cuba. It was in that context that they became internationally known.

Castañeda is correct in observing that during this first period many intellectuals of the left, especially in Europe, invented a Cuba that fit their preferences and priorities.[7] When they felt their ideal tropical socialism was growing authoritarian, when their vision of a wondrous and magical armed struggle seemed to be coming apart, they grew disenchanted.

Reactions to the Soviet intervention in Czechoslovakia in 1968 revealed the distance between the Cuban logic about socialism in the Third World and the Eurocentric logic of that other left. The European left grew up in a continent divided into rival blocs and in the shadow of the traumas of Stalinism, whereas the Cuban left had lived through the Bay of Pigs and the missile crisis.[8] When Fidel Castro made his speech about Czechoslovakia, the Eurocentric left heard only the part that accepted the Soviet intervention as an act of political realism, and not his commentary on that act. From a Cuban point of view, a Soviet intervention in defense of an Eastern European government was susceptible to political explanation to the extent that this same logic would be applied to the whole socialist camp, not only to Europe. Cuba understood the principle of socialist internationalism to be universal, to include revolutionary movements and governments in the Third World, the Cuban Revolution among them. The reference point of Cuban logic in 1968 was the war in Vietnam, where the USSR held back from applying that principle on the basis of the tactical accord between the superpowers that ended the missile crisis of 1962.[9]

The challenge to the Soviets contained in Fidel's speech, calling them to account for their lack of support for socialist revolutions in the Third World, was ignored by the speech's critics—as it still is by those who raise the subject today. The honeymoon between the European intellectual left and Cuba (and between some Latin Americans and Cuba as well) ended with the end of the Prague Spring. But the deeper causes of this disagreement were, to put it one way, more structural than conjunctural.

The claim that the Cuban government adopted a Soviet line in 1968–70 is not sustained by a close look at history. Those years were the moment of greatest distance between the two countries before the era that led to the end of the USSR. The Soviet formula affected Cuba only later—and when that happened, the effect was not a uniform one, either on Cuba's international stance or on all aspects of the Cuban system at home. However much emphasis may be placed on Cuba's imitation of the Soviet model after 1972, the specific path followed by the Cuban process in the 1970s cannot be reduced to that imitation. Further, Castañeda himself recognizes that the Cuban process maintained its attraction for many Latin American countries as it consolidated itself after the 1970s. The domestic dimension—the extent to which the imitations of "real socialism" affected the Cuban system, culture, and thought—is something that perhaps we can adequately assess only now.[10]

The positions of the left with respect to Cuba have always come in varying shades. In general, Latin American intellectuals have presented a rather blurry image of the island, thanks to a lack of information and especially of perceptions from within Cuba itself; paradoxically, this missing piece has become the common denominator of Cuba's image in the world. Those who try to keep up with what is happening in Cuba, and who sympathize with the revolution, have on the whole preferred not to present their criticisms publicly, which does not exactly mean that they are blind to our defects. Some, with more or less knowledge, have decided to voice their critical opinions openly. Among them there are those who still believe in the possibility that the Cuban process will go forward, while others have joined the nihilist ranks of the "second-thoughters," repenting their membership in the left. What all these and other currents seem to me to have in common—from those who justify everything we do, to those who reject us out of hand as "totalitarian"—is a tendency to see and react to Cuba through the prism of their own experiences and national contexts.

Nonetheless, and with all its deficiencies, the Cuban experience continues to be the only revolutionary power and the only anticapitalist experience that managed to consolidate itself in the region, and this makes it a necessary point of reference for the left. If Latin American leftist intellectuals can no longer cite the Cuban model as an archetype—especially in a period when Cuba is merely trying to survive, without pretending to be a model of anything—still the majority of them do not find it fitting to forswear an emblem of popular movements in the region, one whose impact extends beyond the sphere of recognition by governments or by the cultural powers that be.

Castañeda's book reflects in exemplary fashion this problematic state of consciousness, especially as it has been sharpened by the end of socialism in Eastern Europe and the USSR. This is a crisis affecting not only ideological paradigms but the entire culture of the left. Its impact in Cuba is clear, and the vibrations extend beyond the intellectual sector.

But the Cuban situation has its unique ingredients that affect Cuba's culture in general and the political role of its intellectuals in particular. These ingredients must be examined closely and with care.

Intellectuals and Politics

In the eyes of some observers, Cuban intellectuals renounced their role when they identified with the political vanguard that led the triumph and consolidation of the revolution. That political vanguard, although as a group it did not distinguish itself by its theoretical fertility, did assume the role of an intellectual vanguard to the extent that it produced a rupture with old dogmas and an opening to new visions of national and international realities.

The double role of Cuban revolutionary vanguard in the 1960s was a reality even though this revolution's leading nucleus (as opposed to that of the 1930s) included hardly any intellectuals doubling as political leaders. Many of the most prestigious Cuban writers and artists of the 1950s had chosen exile or kept to the margins of political activity. In 1959, however, the majority of the intellectuals fully embraced the political and ideological agenda of the revolution, conscious as they were of the importance of the process for the nation as a whole, not only for the sphere of high culture. They identified with the vanguard and with the revolutionary system, believed in it, and assumed it as their own. As in so many previous historical cases, from Aristotle and Virgil through Hobbes and Verlaine to Diego Rivera and Ernesto Cardenal, they supported a regime and a social order, but especially they supported a sense of recovery of the nation and the homeland that the revolution had brought about.

In the early 1960s, intellectuals' participation in ideological debate was accepted as a legitimate part of the revolutionary cultural order. The intense controversies about conceptions of political culture carried out in the pages of *La Gaceta de Cuba*, the newspaper *Hoy*, or the weekly *Lunes de Revolución*, or the debates about socialist economic theory that unfolded in *Nuestra Industria*, *Cuba Socialista*, and other journals reflected the spirit of this period. The notion that intellectuals should devote themselves to art and literature and not meddle in ideology was rarer than it is for some today. During those intense years, Cubans tried to rise to the ideological creativity of the moment.

Nonetheless, neither then nor in the three decades that followed did an intellectual leadership as such arise. The political vanguard set the terms of debate, including those of intellectual content, in areas ranging from the reinterpretation of Cuban history to ideas about imperialism, Latin Americanism, and revolutionary culture. This phenomenon had multiple causes. Among those that have been suggested are: the particular historical trajectory of the Cuban Revolution, the majority of the intellectuals' conscious alignment with and acceptance of the ideological authority of the revolutionary leadership, the ultimate importance of political decisions in ideological and cultural debates, and other, later factors that began to rigidify cultural life and restrict the reproduction of ideas. The codification of the revolution's ideology and its official incarnation in the state under the particular conditions created by the unceasing U.S. siege narrowed the spaces for diversification of teaching, schools of thought, interpretations, and homegrown modes of viewing culture and ideology. Without a sufficiently large or autonomous space in the mass media or a dynamic role in higher education, the outstanding figures of Cuban culture, despite all their capacity and prestige, have not been able to exercise the sort of moral and ideological influence or authority that would leave its mark on public opinion or in the configuration of referents and diverse currents of thinking, in the way such an influence was historically exercised by Enrique José Varona or the intellectuals of the generation of 1930.

The absence today of such an intellectual leadership and of the conditions that would nurture it—in an historical period very different from the 1960s—limits the rise of new models and referents for culture and social thought in Cuba. That limitation affects not only the cultural dynamic but also the field of ideology. It must be seen within the context of a powerful cultural transformation which took place at the level of the whole society and considerably enlarged the intellectual sector. In social terms, the emergence of new generations of intellectuals from the 1960s on had a truly organic character, organic in the original Gramscian sense, not only in the sense that they self-identified with the revolution. What occurred was a wave of upward mobility as the children of urban and rural workers gained access to the universities.[11] Thus, the group of intellectual figures that represented Cuban culture in 1959 has been converted, by now, into a larger and broader sector of Cuban society that includes diverse generations and specialists in fields from the arts and literature to social and technical sciences.[12]

If in Cuba the intellectuals are not seen as the privileged depository of the social function of critical consciousness, still culture does constitute a fundamental space for the critical discussion of national problems. In such a space, intellectuals should exercise an important function. In various periods institutions such as Casa de las Américas, the Film Institute, and more recently UNEAC[13] have played notable roles in organizing and promoting the opinions, feelings, and participation of Cuban artists and writers. Still, no mechanisms have emerged to give intellectuals an influence in national politics that would make full use of their capacities.

The fact is that the state of consciousness among Cuban intellectuals should not represent a problem for Cuban politicians. According to a recent study, intellectuals are characterized by high interest in participating in the social project, combining an elevated consciousness of their political commitment with a strong critical accent.[14] Their main criticisms address the application of mechanisms that rein in the spirit of creative work and encourage such negative phenomena as inefficiency, mediocrity, fraud, and hypocrisy. Their political worries (such as concern over social deformations like bureaucracy and corruption) predominate over economic ones (such as more immediate necessities). In comparison with findings for other social groups, the intellectuals display a higher level of worry about the future, and a greater stress on the need for interchange with the intellectual community at an international level.[15]

Some aspects of intellectuals' and politicians' mutual images evoke the problems of "real socialism." Most disturbing from the point of view of the intellectuals is to be summoned to political participation and ideological struggle on the one hand, while on the other they are restricted in their role as a factor in shaping social consciousness. Their insufficient access to the communications media and the limited role of debate over ideas in higher education attest to this.

That the Latin American country with the broadest and most organic layer of professionals and technicians does not provide them with a larger presence in the interchange of ideas and the formation of public opinion is an incongruity. But this incongruity results from systemic defects in the areas of education, science, culture, and ideology, not merely from circumstantial deviations in the political sphere.

These defects stem in part from an identification of unity with unanimity.[16] The Cuban concept of unity has been based on its continuous strategic necessity for the defense of the national project, but the "unanimist" interpretation reflects a distortion of that concept. Given this interpretation, many sectors and layers of society do not yet enjoy sufficient degrees of participation and effective presence in the ideological channels of the system, nor instruments (institutions and mass media) that will always guarantee their full exercise. The intellectuals are among these sectors, although the same could be said of women or of youth. A deeper socialist concept of democracy could offer civil society, including the intellectuals and their institutions, greater access to the channels where ideology is shaped.

One phenomenon sharply reflecting such problems is the separation among artistic-literary production, social science, higher education, and political thought. The Cuban intellectual movement's growing consciousness of this alienation has been emerging under the conditions of the Special Period. In an apparently paradoxical way—although perhaps responding to an implacable logic of social consciousness—the deficient communication among these fields is all the more urgently evident in the midst of crisis, as is the need to capitalize on intelligence as part of the solution of national problems.[17] Nonetheless, a cultural integration that realizes the potential of this capital is still lacking.

These are not the only incongruities. Mutual suspicion between the realms of politics and culture has been, as suggested above, a characteristic trait. Policymakers have not always expressed sufficient receptivity to intellectual projects, especially those of the younger generation.[18] Intellectuals have charged the bureaucracy with underestimating the political, social, and psychological value of artistic culture and of the sciences not associated with material production.[19] The paternalistic habits that have characterized some styles of leadership in many spheres are not absent from the terrain of culture and ideology.

Just as some political figures fail to see culture as anything but a means of mobilization, or to understand the social role of the intellectuals, certain intellectuals consider politics to be a totally alien zone and remain incapable of setting foot outside their own realm or of grasping the logic and problems of any other one. This limitation keeps them from seeing that, as Graziella Pogolotti has said, politics too is one of the zones of culture.

Others, by contrast, demand a high political profile as if they deserved it simply for belonging to the intellectual sector or coming from a new generation—independent of their capacities, talents, and creativity. This naive vision of the political importance of the intellectual is the other side of the coin of their having been undervalued by the bureaucracy.

Finally, some intellectuals display a refractory attitude toward what they perceive as the discourse or political culture "of the left." That phenomenon—not limited, of course, to intellectuals—demands a separate treatment because of its multiple ramifications and what it reveals about our national problems.

The Ideological Crisis as a Cultural Problem

The fall of the socialist camp has brought a change in the world ideological context, and both events have had their effects in Cuba. One effect is that the discourse of the left no longer has such an organic place in the society nor is it viewed with the same presumption of legitimacy as before. In 1950 Isaac Deutscher wrote in a text of surprising currency, "The ex-communist intellectual . . . no longer throws out the dirty water of the . . . revolution to protect the baby; he discovers that the baby is a monster which must be strangled. The heretic becomes a renegade."[20] In Cuba some intellectuals—including some who never were heretics—now renounce ideas rather than revising them. Left-wing values, concepts, and approaches tend to be perceived as antiquated, anachronistic, and insufficient to the task of understanding a culture that is postmodern, total, and impregnable.

This break is in fact one more symptom of the ills of "real socialism." The ex-communist, as Deutscher goes on to say, is characterized by "narrow-mindedness . . . he remains a sectarian. He is an inverted Stalinist. . . . Having once been caught by the 'greatest illusion,' he is now obsessed by the greatest disillusionment of our time. His former illusion at least assumed a positive ideal. His disillusionment is wholly negative."[21] From this disillusion develops a language that classifies both real socialism and fascist dictatorships under the undifferentiated label "totalitarianism."[22]

These victims of disillusionment, a friend said to me recently in less literary language, are like baseball fans who suddenly decide to root for a different club because their team lost the World Series. Still, the ex-communist syndrome has other causes, as Deutscher implied. One of the most evident is the practice of a scholastic, catechistic, dogmatic Marxism, which ceased to represent an intellectually creative position in Cuba long before the fall of socialism in Europe. Several generations of Cubans were educated in this Marxism.[23]

Dogmatism is a hyperstructured representation of thought which always leads to a tautology; nothing new is ever learned, the rules are only confirmed once again. It is a kind of fundamentalism that expects social reality to follow the models in books.[24] Dogmatism permits evasion of the task of developing concrete knowledge about concrete reality. The social sciences, for instance, are limited to reaffirming the inevitable course of history—even if history has gone in the least-imagined direction. Despite certain peculiar local contributions, we can still say with assurance that dogmatic Marxism in Cuba imitated the East, accepting its presuppositions, logic, and implications. Although the nucleus of Cuban revolutionary ideology has always been, to a large degree, antithetical to dogma,[25] still there have been those who have tried to reduce it to a textbook of learned and immutable truths.

The tendency to confuse left-wing thinking with dogmatism, therefore, is the sequel to the prevalence of such dogmatic schema in Cuban political and intellectual education. This confusion characteristically shows itself in the labeling of expressions considered conservative, inflexible, closed, or simplistic as "left-wing"—which is a contradiction in terms, because the banners of the left are, by definition, the opposite: social change, breaking with traditional models, challenging accepted truths, confronting conservatism and isolationism, renewing intellectual projects, and defending the ideals of progress, democracy, participation, and liberation. The left-wing current in Cuba comes from Felix Varela and from Luz, through José Martí, the Group of Thirteen, and the Nuestro Tiempo society; it symbolizes the intellectual vanguard, authenticity, and heterodoxy, and it is fundamental to our cultural tradition. Such a heritage demands a rigorous reading of Cuba's present and of its true situation in the contemporary world, a reading superior to the parochial commonplaces[26] and the authoritarianism that characterize impoverished versions of the left.

This confusion of terms so diametrically opposed as "left" and "conservatism" may stem, however, from the existence of truly conservative elements in the political culture of the revolutionary period.

The conservatism that crept into the political culture of the period has its own modes of reproduction. It is natural for an interest in preserving social conquests to bring with it a certain amount of worry about changes[27]—especially after the cataclysms in Eastern Europe put the idea of the reversibility of socialism in circulation. But even before that concern arose, paternalism, styles of leadership and education, and stereotyped systematization of ideology had jelled into conservative visions of social consciousness.

That effect is related to a phenomenon reaching beyond the strictly intellectual or theoretical arena, affecting the ideological fabric of the society as a whole. Political education has been seen as little more than the illustration of an ideological speech. Among the weaknesses of such political education, besides dogmatic Marxism, are deficient teaching of Cuban history and devaluation of socialist ideology through the use of schematic forms of propaganda and uncreative use of the mass media.[28]

In a situation as difficult as the present one, the rupture of external ideological isolation demands a confrontation with the circles of anti-Cuban propaganda and a debate with critics of many stripes.[29] This is turn requires domestic debate, since that battle cannot be won with slogans, only with ideas. As the 1993 UNEAC National Congress recognized, "Confrontation between ideas is part of the nature of intellectual work and an irreplaceable stimulus for its development."[30] To be effective, moreover, such debate needs to extend beyond the living rooms (or rooftops) of intellectuals and the cubicles of experts.

The intellectuals' duty is to contribute actively to this task, according to their own capacities, from clear and unambiguous positions.

The social and humanistic sciences, the arts, and intellectuals in general could contribute to the search for new clues and new paths—not so much in order to tell the politicians what they ought to do, as to foresee and confront problems. Especially in the social field, intellectual capacity might contribute to an understanding of national and international phenomena—to dissecting the new situation and its social, political, and ideological ingredients, as well to seeking out its implications for a new model of development. This becomes even truer when we realize that discussions of the crisis and the model involve more than purely economic considerations. The multiplication of tensions within the structure of Cuban social relations is now reflected in a crisis of social conscience and consciousness, in both ideological and ethical terms. There is no way to carry out a profound analysis of this crisis, nor even to discuss the parameters of a new model, without viewing that model as a whole.[31]

"In such difficult times . . ."

"In such difficult times, when we face so many threats . . . and culture is the first thing that must be saved,"[32] it is necessary to understand what the strategic significance of culture is.

In an earlier section of this essay I referred to tensions between political figures and intellectuals—or, better put, between their respective social roles. Still, there are many and promising spaces in which they may come together. Without turning culture into an instrument, politics can take intelligent advantage of culture's enormous power to facilitate the realization of common goals. Above all, politics can interact with culture and learn from it, because culture has certain strong points that admit of no substitutes.

The strategic value of culture operates by way of multiple definitions and functions.

In an anthropological sense, culture includes all social activity. Under current conditions of ideological confusion, bombardment by propaganda, socioeconomic readjustment, and the devaluation of discourse, culture represents a plane of communication and a referent that, though differentiated and pluralistic, is fundamentally held in common.

As a space in which different generations and social groups may meet, culture allows national values and interests to be brought up to date; it offers depth and contemporary meaning to national unity. As an expression of knowledge and self-consciousness, political culture has virtues that, despite all ideological uncertainties, are essential for these times.

From a political point of view, culture represents a system of resistence to forces that break down social cohesion. To borrow from the language of biology, we can say that such pathologies, both external and internal, grow more virulent in times like these. There are no more effective mechanisms for neutralizing the invasion of antigens of the (post)modern world, and for repairing dysfunctions in our own system, than those provided by the many facets of culture. In their response to foreign and hostile entities, cultural products act according to the principles of immunity, not as the kind of ideological condom whose ineffectiveness is well known. Culture can generate a more trustworthy system of antibodies and bodily repair.

But this biological metaphor—which is just that, and should not be seen as a functionalist approach to culture—does not fully describe the intellectuals' task. What is fundamental is for them to truly understand the challenges of globalization and be able to offer options for a response. They must not limit themselves to pointing out the magnitude of the difficulties, but rather, to put it one way, must contribute to ensuring that the baby doesn't drown in the cold water of its first bath. Therefore they must develop a profound understanding of the contradictions that maintain the body politic (and social) in tension. To do this, to expose the stubborn dynamic of national problems and the contradictory ways of the new globalism, requires a richer and more rational vision of the situation, one that can neutralize the discourse of "common sense"[33] prevailing within the tunnel vision of daily life.

Naturally this represents a great responsibility. If politicians are obligated to keep their ears to the ground, even more so are the intellectuals who seek to interpret the problems of their social environment. In this way, they can contribute to a more faithful representation of that environment, to rendering the Cuban profile—or, better, profiles—in their true and contemporary dimensions.

Finally, culture has a use value, and therefore an exchange value as well. But the political economy of culture cannot be reduced to the market. Culture's strong and productive role consists not only of the products of art and science becoming merchandise, but of satisfying some of humankind's basic needs. The need to think and to know, to imagine and to create value is what can distinguish a worker from a consumer, a citizen from a client, a *real* person from a merely *instrumental* one. This is a social difference, not a "subjective" or "spiritual" one. If we do not want the worker to become *homo economicus,* the great economic decisions must be evaluated carefully and integrally, which is to say socially.

For this cooperation between culture and politics to develop, however, we must recognize that the most important problems confronting Cuban culture at the moment are of necessity the same major problems confronting the nation. In other words, any cultural debate about the present and the future is political as well.

In this cultural capacity to invent the future lies—still, surely—the force and significance of what some have called the Cuban utopia.[34] Rather than of utopias, "armed" or "unarmed," I prefer to speak of ideals, a more common term in our cultural and political tradition, which should not be confused with chimeras, or vague dreams, or ideological stereotypes. I refer to the great political and social ideals that have shaped the nation and, to quote the maestro, José Martí, built the most important trenches, which are "more valuable than trenches of stone."

RAÚL CAÑIBANO (1961–) worked as a welder until 1993, when he became a free-lance photographer. His artwork has been exhibited in Cuba, Latin America, Europe, Japan, Canada, and the United States, and published in *Asahicamera* (Japan, 1997), *Muestra de Fotografía Latinoamericana* (Mexico, 1996), *100 Años de Fotografía Cubana* (Spain, 1999), and other books. He was awarded first prize at the 1995 Bienal de Fotografía Contemporanea in Havana.

1. Portable altar devoted to Afro-Cuban deity San Lázaro/Babalú Ayé crossing the street in front of Havana's Central Park.

2. Independence War general Calixto
García looking north on seaside at
Malecón. This art photo evokes themes
of race and national independence.

3. José Martí bust behind old North American car and passing child. Most foreign reporters are fascinated only by the second element.

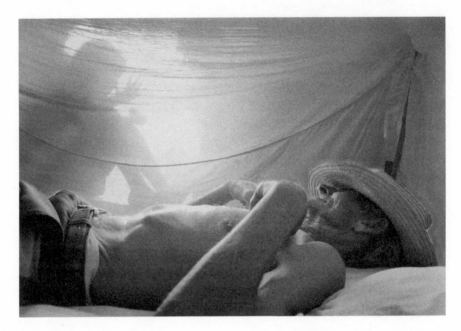

4. Old cane cutter taking a nap.

5. Transvestite performer posing for
photographer. Public performance
of transvestite shows, as well as other
previously taboo artistic subjects, are
increasingly common.

6. Self-employed charcoal producer in the Ciénaga de Zapata, a member of the increasingly populous sector of private farmers.

7. Young cane cutter at rest. The old dream of escaping from sugar dependence may be closer than ever to fulfillment.

8. Jesus, a *santero*, and San Lázaro/Babalú
Ayé at the entrance of a Roman Catholic
church on Calle Reina. The Catholic
Church still refuses to recognize syncretic
religious practices.

9. Oldster on rollerskates. The elderly
constitute an increasing share of the
Cuban population.

HUMBERTO MAYOL (1960–), with long experience as a photo reporter for several Cuban and Venezuelan newspapers, has won prizes for his artwork in Cuba (National Press Photography Exhibit), Poland, and Japan (UNESCO, 1993). His photos have been shown in solo exhibitions in Cuba, Germany, Paraguay, Brazil, Spain, Italy, Venezuela, Ecuador, and the United States, and published in *100 Años de Fotografía Cubana* (Spain, 1999), *Fotofest Catalogue* (Houston, 1994, 1996), and other books. He works as a freelance photographer in Havana.

10. Trio of farmers. New forms of agricultural cooperatives, replacing state farms, have offered new incentives for agricultural production.

11. Couple on Havana seawall. His shirt reads "Election ballot. February 24 [anniversary of outbreak of 1895 war of independence]. Candidates: 1. Fatherland. 2. Revolution. 3. Socialism."

12. Traditional Cuban living room. Nationalist, socialist, and religious images very often mix with popular culture elements, like the life-size doll.

13. Fidel Castro, still a very energetic human being.

14. Self-employed snack vendor with ads
for self-employed photographer upstairs.

15. Crowded bus. Public transportation,
though improving, is still difficult.

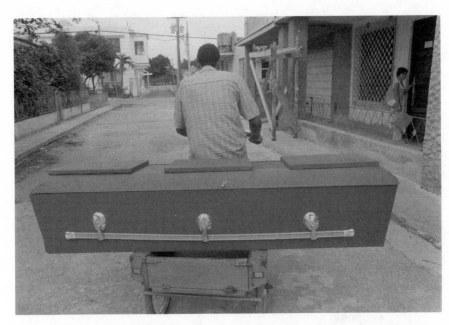

16. Coffin on bicycle cart. The Special
Period imposed heavy pressures on both
life and death.

17. Street demonstration. Public mobilizations continue to be part of Cuban political participation.

18. Pope John Paul II's public address in
the Plaza de la Revolución, Havana,
January 1998.

ROLANDO PUJOL (1954–) has worked as a photo reporter for the major Cuban newspapers and magazines, as well as for the tourism industry and the military. His photos covering Cuban cities, culture, the environment, politics, and entertainment have been published in Cuba, Spain, Great Britain, and other countries. Solo exhibitions of his artwork have been held in Mexico and Turkey. He was awarded the Premio Nacional de Periodismo in 1988. He works in Havana as a freelance photographer for advertising companies and the tourism industry.

19. Wedding during a hurricane.

20. State ration store, New Year's Eve.

21. Sleeping cashier. The economic crisis affected the supply of goods in the state sector during the 1990s.

22. Cuban inventiveness: repairing an old car.

23. Shoppers. Lining up to buy products
and services continues to be part of daily
life and culture.

24. "Don't buy in a hurry." The state
sector is challenged by ever-increasing
consumer demand.

25. Student rally. Members of the new
Cuban generation have grown up in
conditions strikingly different from those
of their parents.

26. Swimming in the rain. Hurricanes, heavy rains, and droughts are ever present in the Cuban environment.

27. Children in the Paseo del Prado, Havana. Foreign visitors always comment on the racial heterogeneity and comfort of Cuban street life.

28. Woman eating ice cream, Calle 23, Havana.

29. Hoisting drinking water to an upstairs
apartment.

30. Cuban rock-and-roll enthusiasts at the traditional summer Carnival.

31. Militiamen and militiawomen dancing
in the street during Carnival.

32. Informal elderly aerobics class.

33. "Yankees, stop fucking with us!
[Construction workers] Brigade # 26."
Demonstration in the Plaza de la
Revolución, Havana.

34. Woman with her spaghetti ration from
a state store, Old Havana.

ENRIQUE DE LA UZ (1944–) has worked as a professional photographer for *Cuba Internacional, Bohemia, Revolución y Cultura,* and other leading Cuban magazines. His artwork has been shown since 1970 in numerous venues in Cuba and abroad, such as the Museo Nacional de Bellas Artes and the Fototeca de Cuba and galleries in Spain and Switzerland. It also appears in books on Cuban and Latin American photography including *Canto a la realidad* and *100 Años de Fotografía Cubana.* A film and art critic and a documentary filmmaker, he works as a freelance photographer and is president of the art photo section of the Unión Nacional de Escritores y Artistas de Cuba.

35. Arriving in town from the countryside for a street festival. Punta Alegre, a small town in the north of Ciego de Ávila province.

36. Bicycle taxi. Cubans use this new
phenomenon to meet all sorts of needs.
Cumanayagua, Cienfuegos province.

37. Buying draft beer. Customers provide
their own receptacles. Cumanayagua,
Cienfuegos province.

38. Young people at a street festival.
Globalized culture and its symbols reach
even small towns like this. Cumanayagua,
Cienfuegos province.

39. Religious procession in the streets—
a recent reappearance of an old practice.
Cumanayagua, Cienfuegos province.

40. Garage door with patriotic slogan and Cuban flag. Punta Alegre, Ciego de Ávila province.

Civil Society and Politics in the 1990s

Civil Society and National Politics

Aside from the international factors—the disintegration of the socialist camp and the end of the USSR—that in the 1990s brought the beginning of a new historical period in the Cuban revolutionary process, there were also domestic factors that marked a turning point. In the terrain of politics, the new dynamic was reflected in a change in the relationship between the state and civil society.

One of the most significant documents of recent years, the *Granma* editorial of September 2, 1989, expressed it this way:

> What is most important is that the whole society and the whole Party must draw lessons and reflections from these bitter events. . . . Perhaps in the future these occurrences that have shocked the country can be seen as the turning point toward a profound institutional, political, and moral improvement of the Revolution.
>
> . . . It is necessary to admit that deeper social problems lie beneath what has occurred. We cannot be satisfied with the simplification that attributes all problems of this type to a lack of control. . . .
>
> We have to seek true solutions in a coherent improvement of the country's institutions. . . . In what has occurred there is present a group of defects which, in one way or another, involves all the institutions of the Revolution. . . .
>
> . . . A serious self-analysis should lead us to the idea that improvement in the society includes the functioning of the Party, which is not only a subject but also an object of rectification. . . .

Security, in a country like Cuba, is above all an ideological and political question. . . . It involves something much more ambitious. That is the unity between the people and the Revolution. That is confidence in the men who exercise power.

The international and domestic changes that began in 1989 caused an evolution in the conditions under which our politics are carried out. The dynamic of the society with respect to the state began to enter a qualitatively new phase not caused solely by the economic crisis. This dynamic has left its mark on both ideology and consensus, two central aspects in the carrying out of politics.

Why do we try, nonetheless, to avoid observing things from the standpoint of civil society?

The narrowness of the paradigms through which the Cuban experience has been conceptualized, the scarcity of serious empirical studies, and the prevalence of stereotypes about the political system have all contributed to erasing real society from our researchers' field of view.

Two factors, especially, have affected the image of civil society. The first has been the weakness of Cuban social science. The second is the persistence of an image that identifies society with political system and reduces the political system to the Party and the figure of Fidel Castro. In the realm of political sociology, there is a tendency to ignore the existence of civil society as such in Cuba. Parodoxically, there are those within Cuba whose views, with respect to this overly exclusive vision, coincide with some Cuban studies undertaken abroad by an opposite ideological camp.

Now that the concept of civil society has come into vogue, it has become entangled in a web of theoretical confusion, biased interpretations, and ideological distortion. Among the resulting stereotypes, for instance, is the idea that civil society constitutes an ideologically neutral sphere separated from politics. The essence of civil society is defined as equality, and therefore it becomes the foundation of democracy. Although civil society may contain new sources of legitimization and areas of consensus that the state needs to take into consideration, still we must remember that it is the realm of pluralism, and therefore of inequality. The notion that its actors exist outside the contradictory world of ideology is an illusion.

The ideological distortion of the concept becomes evident when civil society is viewed as a tool for destabilizing the political system. In fact, pluralism in Cuba has an often overlooked sociological basis. Since 1959 the reproduction of Cuban social structure and classes has evolved from a situation of simple relations between classes to a more complex situation characterized by their internal differentiation. Despite the opinion of some authors to the contrary, this pluralism has not been imposed by certain social actors, but by the social dynamic itself. The rise of diversified ideological expressions may be explained, in large part, as a result of a process of social differentiation. To attribute this dynamic to exterior pressures or to actors such as the "human rights groups" reveals a propensity to privilege conspiracy theories as a more powerful paradigm for explaining change than the sociology of social structure.

Another widespread stereotype holds that the only Cuban formations that deserve the name "civil society" are the so-called human rights groups or dissident organizations, and the Catholic church.

Non-Marxist Cuban sociology had already demonstrated that Cuban popular religion is not exactly Catholic.[1] At the level of civil society, the most widespread Cuban religions of African origin represent a network of relations and social mobilization more important than that of a Catholic church that continues, in its structure, its ideological positions, and its social practice, to be relatively rigid and unrepresentative. Unlike the Catholic Church, Santería does not have a rigid national hierarchy, nor does it answer to the designs of a foreign power like the Vatican. Santería's hierarchies and modes of social organization are rooted in civil society itself, and they operate in a more democratic and popular fashion. If the associations and sites of worship of these popular religions were a breeding ground for political opposition, then the stability of the system would be broadly placed in question.

Insofar as it is possible to make an objective characterization of the so-called human rights groups, it seems evident that they should more properly be called political opposition groups. They form and divide in such a fashion that it is difficult to refer to them as a defined sector, much less to see any connection between them and Cuban civil society. In other words, they do not represent any given social groups whose rights might have been infringed in some way, such as, for instance, Cubans of African origin, or religious believers, or women. Their agendas are lacking in the social content that might be expected of human rights groups in other countries. Their platforms are eminently political and may be summarized as opposition to the system. Nonetheless, apart from "being in opposition," these agendas do not reveal an ideological identity. They run the gamut from "the defense of human rights" through "an opening in the system," "a Cuban perestroika," "saving the country," "peaceful civic resistance," and "the return of the exiles," to "using culture as a common path in the search for the true solution to save the fatherland of all." Their most common feature seems to be the contrast between their notoriety abroad and their lack of true presence in Cuban civil society itself.

In comparison to human rights groups in other countries of the region, the Cuban groups may be distinguished by their declared political connotation; they represent either inorganic *focos* of opposition or vehicles for emigration.

Civil Society and Inter-American Relations

Today the concept of civil society is closely entwined with international relations. An example close at hand can be seen in the documents of the recent Summit of the Americas.[2]

The Action Plan approved by the Miami summit contains recommendations for the "strengthening, effective exercise, and consolidation of democracy."[3] These include strengthening the role of civil society in the public politics of the hemisphere. The Plan declares that "a democracy is judged by the rights enjoyed by its least influential members"[4] and that "a strong and diverse civil society" is one that can affect "the management and oversight of resources" through "broad participation in public issues."[5]

An analysis of how this description relates to Cuba will reveal the true role of democracy in the hemispheric initiative announced by the Summit.

We must begin by distinguishing between the position taken about the desirability of changes in Cuba, the real connotation of the term "democracy" in the current hemispheric situation, and the interests and objectives promoted by the various international actors.

The nature of the Cuban political order is not of much concern to the civil societies of the Americas. To a great extent, the social movements of the hemisphere tend to recognize Cuba's merits in the area of basic rights, regardless of their ideological sympathies or preferences. The policies of economic embargo and isolation imposed by the United States are not supported by a popular consensus even in the United States itself. Diverse social sectors throughout the Americas, including entrepreneurs, churches, NGOs, and important national figures, including public officials, have openly called for a reintegration of Cuba into the hemisphere and the revocation of measures intended to isolate the Cuban regime. Many figures whose political positions are far from socialist hold that this change would contribute more to promoting the transformations they would like to see on the island than would maintaining the premise that a democratic opening can be forced on a country like Cuba by means of isolation.

Likewise, Cuban civil society itself does not seem to have been taken much into account. Instruments like those of U.S. policy toward Cuba— the embargo, hostility, threats, and extreme ideologization—contradict the goal of "fostering understanding, dialogue and political reconciliation, at the request of the affected state and bearing in mind that national reconciliation comes from within."[6]

The policy of external pressure has been counterproductive to the extent that it has stimulated conservatism in Cuba; it has permitted those resistant to change to appeal to the argument that Cuban national interests are weakened by implementing policies that could be perceived as concessions to outside pressures, particularly from the United States.

The net result has been that Cuba's external policies are more open, pluralist, and flexible than its domestic ones.

In spite of the fact that some in Cuba prefer wholesale rejection of any language and concepts that do not match the traditional Cuban discourse, the position taken by Cuba during the Cartagena Summit, in June of 1994, was different. Fidel Castro said: "Cuba regards the Northamerican idea of convoking the NGOs of the continent to produce recommendations for an agenda as a positive one. But all must be invited. The demands of indigenous peoples, women, peasant organizations, unions, and the other representatives of civil societies must all be heard, without interventionist exclusions, because they all have a lot to say with respect to the issues of this Summit."[7]

The changes that have taken place in Cuba—in its internal situation, the multiplication of actors in its civil society, and the diversification of its political system—could all contribute to resolving the hemispheric problems outlined by the Summit of the Americas in Miami by moving toward a more integral model of democracy and human rights. This approach promotes such causes as popular participation, social justice, equity, national development and stability, with full exercise of all rights—none of which can be separated from the question of democracy itself.[8]

The network of intrahemispheric interests that come into play in relation to Cuba goes beyond the level of ideology. The Summit project includes both protagonists and issues of a transgovernmental nature, such as the private sector and free trade. These may play a more influential role in hemispheric change than the governments themselves, plagued as the governments are by insecurity and fragility of consensus.

In a context of economic instability, in the midst of conditions that make for abrupt and unpredictable crises even within political and economic systems heretofore regarded as solid, the case of Cuba does not—in spite of the gravity of Cuba's depression—turn out to be a phenomenon foreign to those that the southern part of the hemisphere is experiencing. Although Cuba is not a crucial matter on the inter-American agenda, not a matter over which the United States or Latin America and the Caribbean are disposed to risk vital interests, Cuba does represent a sort of mirror of the past and future of interhemispheric relations. On the one hand, it suggests an echo of the Cold War and the unresolved vacuum of the post–Cold War era. On the other hand, Cuba represents a social project larger than itself, which other civil societies in the hemisphere are also pursuing. No political system in the hemisphere can afford to ignore it.

6

Toward a New Socialist Society?

Changes, Crisis, and Social Configurations in Cuba

Most internationally circulated discussions of a transition in Cuba share at least two premises. The first is that the issue in question is a political change from socialism to capitalism, similar to that which occurred in the countries of Eastern Europe. The second is that substantive transformations worthy of being termed a change will take place only after the government of Fidel Castro comes to an end.

Neither of these premises can muster much evidence on its behalf. To the contrary, it is possible to see and to show that a dynamic of change has been under way on the island for more than a decade, a dynamic that has been transforming not only the economy but social relations, political context, and culture in a significant way.

Symptoms of exhaustion of the Cuban model of development were evident in the mid-1980s. In the functioning of the economy, they were reflected in such indicators as declining growth rates, low labor productivity, overemployment in state enterprises, excessive centralization and bureaucratization of government agencies, high import dependency, rising foreign debt, and deficits in both state budget and international balances.[1]

These symptoms of economic stagnation matched a social structure that had lost its old dynamism and upward mobility while accumulating problems of internal differentiation, sectoral disproportion, and others such as the insufficient representation of youth, blacks, and women in the power structure.[2] The political system suffered from a decline in the quality of citizen participation, less effective action by the representative bodies of People's Power,[3] a swollen management apparatus, and formalism and inertia in the mechanisms for rising through the ranks. Finally, the communications media and social thought showed a tendency to repeat patterns of propaganda and formulas characteristic of Soviet socialism.

Beginning in 1986, the policy known as *rectificación* inaugurated a review of the assumptions of this model, even before Soviet perestroika would change the direction of "real socialism." The third and fourth congresses of the Cuban Communist Party, held in 1986 and 1991, hosted a critical debate on these problems, but the political process of rectification went deeper than those particular events. It was expressed in the public discussions that took place throughout the country in 1989–90 around the document known as the Call to the Fourth Party Congress. From this debate, which was the broadest and most democratic known in Cuba in recent decades, emerged an agenda of national needs to be addressed. These included:

- in the economic system, further differentiation allowing nonstate forms of property and control, such as mixed, cooperative, and private businesses within a socialist framework

- greater public participation in the political process, not only to elect, consult, and mobilize, but also to make and control decisions

- more decentralization of government and transfer of decision-making power to local and regional levels

- a more effective role for the National Assembly of People's Power in carrying out the affairs of state

- more room for nongovernmental activity, from churches to associations

- redefinition of the goals of the socialist system, such as equality, social justice, sovereignty, and development

- leaving behind styles and mechanisms of bureaucratic control over cultural expression, social thought, and ideological debate

In the midst of this process, the fall of the Berlin Wall adversely affected both the government and the people of Cuba. The collapse of socialism in Eastern Europe, the dismantling of the Comecon economic bloc, and the later crumbling of the USSR occurred at a crucial time for the process of renewal and transformation that was developing in Cuba. Separated from its lines of credit, markets, and sources of supply, the Cuban economy declined between 35 percent and 50 percent from 1991 to 1993. The sense of isolation, abandonment, instability, and especially the impact of this decline on all aspects of daily life had a devastating effect. The abrupt cutoff of Soviet military aid deepened the sense of exposure, of vulnerability to the threat emanating from the United States. The discrediting of a bankrupt "real socialism" had an ideological effect, provoking disorientation and the loss of historically created referents for wide sectors of the population.

The responses to such a crisis could not add up to a structured plan with a perfectly programmed repertory of measures. Rather, they developed like the actions of a military campaign of national defense. The title "Special Period in Peacetime" referred to a scenario of minimum resources and maximum austerity which had been imagined for a wartime contingency. In 1993—with one-third less than the necessary supply of petroleum, only half of the normal food imports, more than 60 percent of industry paralyzed, agriculture doing without fertilizers and pesticides, the disappearance of negotiated prices for sugar, nickel, and citrus exports, a lack of public transport, shortages of wheat to make bread and of powdered milk for children—the country hit bottom. Awakening to the post–Cold War world was, for Cubans, like waking into an endless nightmare.

The government attempted to revive state agricultural production, to try out new ways of organizing the workforce, to maintain the past practice of offering only an egalitarian distribution of controlled goods at fixed prices; it tried to resist the opening of free markets, the appearance of middlemen, new rich, and other inequalities; it sought a recovery powered by the engine of tourism and attraction of foreign investment; and it tried, at the same time, to maintain a social policy of full employment without damage to the educational and health systems. Finally the Cuban government learned that it could not achieve its objectives, preserving the gains of the system, without substantial innovation.

The key to these strategic changes was the constitutional reform approved in July 1992, which modified approximately 56 percent of the existing constitution's text. Possibly the most important amendment (without stopping now to discuss the reform's other political-ideological content) was the reconceptualization of the property question.[4] This re-definition allowed for the reversibility of state property, recognizing the possibility of private property in what it characterized as nonfundamental means of production. Similarly, it classified new forms of joint ventures and economic associations, agricultural property, cooperative property, personal property, and the property of mass organizations and social organizations. This reform paved the way for the major pieces of economic legislation that would be adopted in the coming years.

Thus, in the middle of the crisis, what could be defined as a new phase of reform and change in the Cuban economic, social, and political system began.

With its legality established by the constitutional reform, the new policy of broadening and pursuing foreign investment would be restructured in the Foreign Investment Law approved in 1995. Two other measures, promulgated in 1993, marked another important milestone in economic policy: the creation on state-owned land of new cooperatives, known as Basic Units of Cooperative Production (Spanish initials UBPC), thanks to which control of the majority of arable land passed into private hands; and the authorization of self-employment. In 1994 the opening of markets for the sale of farm products and light manufactured goods established legal space for markets with freely fluctuating prices. Finally, between 1995 and 1996, macroeconomic policies known as measures of economic stabilization were established to reduce the monetary overhang through changes in prices and taxes, reduce the number of unnecessary state personnel, and otherwise adjust matters that affected the state budget.

The Sphere of Civil Society

The opening to foreign investment, the conspicuous role of tourism, the rise of self-employment, the redistribution of state lands into private hands, the establishment of the farmers' and industrial markets, the dollarization of the economy, the space filled by the informal economy, the organization of a tax system, and other reform measures have affected preexisting Cuban society as strongly as if they were an act of social engineering.

The economic crisis, in itself, has produced counterproductive effects that are not subject to the strict control of the state or the preferences of the political project. The fall in purchasing power of salaries and the rise of other sources of income; the drop in availability of products in the state stores, growth of the black market, and rise in price of the family "market basket"; the growth of inequality in income distribution and access to hard currency, consumer goods, and work; and the phenomena of corruption and prostitution—all of these left their negative stamp on various social groups' ways of acting and thinking.

The new conditions, partly a consequence of political necessities and partly of the dynamic of the crisis itself, remodeled social space and its cast of actors. At the same time, they affected the established links between society and the state.

One result has been the appearance of new actors who do not depend economically upon the traditional state sphere. Among these new actors are:

- self-employed workers

- private sector agricultural workers (small private owners, cooperative members, individuals who have the right to make use of state-owned land)

- workers in the informal economy

- employees of foreign firms

This private sector is not the only differentiated space in Cuban society. Some other social groups such as the technicians and professionals had already, in the 1980s, developed their particular importance in the social structure.[5] To get an idea of the significance of this sector, consider that in the revolutionary period Cuban universities have graduated half a million students into an economically active population that is currently about four million.

In addition, the sphere of nonstate organizations has changed significantly. Besides the unions, the student organizations, and those of similar sectors, such as women, peasants, and neighbors, there are organizations devoted to groups with special interests whether professional, religious, community, academic, cultural, social, or avocational.[6]

To those institutional spaces we may add others that, strictly speaking, constitute links between the state and civil society. These include the representative bodies of People's Power, the schools, the collective organizations within the workplaces, and even the various levels of the Communist Party, whose size and functions give it some interests beyond those of the state.[7]

Clearly, civil society is not just a realm of economic relations and of pluralism but also a realm of inequality. Neither economic power nor power that derives from the activity of nongovernmental organizations and institutions is equitably divided. The limited opening to market relations, together with distortions brought by the crisis, have given rise to actors who concentrate economic power and to new social relations. They have given rise to hierarchies, attributes, and values that express these social relations, including symbols of success and social preeminence that were previously unknown or unaccepted.

What had earlier been perceived as a deviation from the norm, inconsistent with the prevailing values, and an indicator of corruption or marginality (what the reigning discourse identified as "bourgeoisification"—living off income in dollars, and displaying consumption patterns and styles identifiable as those of capitalist societies) has ceased to be rejected out of hand as offensive to community norms; it has even become a paradigm for some groups.[8] In any case, it has become the attribute of a certain status and a certain quota of power.

Those and other ideological effects run against the grain of socialist discourse. They occur as a consequence of a crisis that is not only economic but affects established values and paradigms. A restoration of the equilibrium between work and compensation, between social prestige and access to social and economic rewards, between merit and personal dedication to work—such a restoration can contribute to overcoming the complex of undesired, negative elements characteristic of this period. For that to occur, however, three things would have to be integrated in a more coherent and stable way: the real economy on which the society rests, the image of the emerging social structure, and the socialist discourse itself.

In this new model of socialism that must take shape in Cuba, we may expect that a high profile of state participation would be maintained, along with other collective and social forms of property. We may expect, at the same time, a greater decentralization of state economic direction in various spheres. Recent tendencies could be projected into the future in the following ways:[9]

- Decentralization and reduction of the central state apparatus
- Maintenance of the state's function of orienting economic activity as a whole, with greater regulatory effectiveness but a smaller administrative role
- Development of a management system for state and joint-venture enterprises that answers to criteria of greater efficiency and the preservation of essential public services
- Continuation of the national system of health, education, and social security with more decentralized and efficient modalities
- Extension of cooperatives and self-management in agriculture and other sectors, which could include workers' control of an eminently collective nature based on social priorities
- Reform of the monetary-financial system including greater control over the money supply, progressive taxes on income and especially on private activity, and circulation of a single, convertible national currency
- End of the black market

In this new environment, beyond the crisis, relations between civil society and state would carve out a new channel. Their final shape would also depend on the effectiveness with which the state could develop its new policies and, in general, reformulate the bases of consensus.

Development of the Cuban Political Model in the 1990s

In spite of the crisis, the pervasive specter of the implosion of Eastern Europe, and the inhibiting effect of renewed U.S. threats to Cuban security and stability, the process of internal change has modified the Cuban political process in important ways.

The policy of rectification, which began (as discussed above) before the end of the Cold War was in sight, formulated an agenda for changing the political and economic system. This agenda included a new way of seeing the relations between state and society, and a new way of thinking about political and social relations within socialism.

The postponement of some of these changes, or their adaptation to the conditions imposed by the crisis, has not eliminated them from the agenda. In fact, in spite of the overwhelming effect unleashed by the changes in Eastern Europe, the economic policy implemented since the constitutional reforms of 1992 shows a will for change that responds to the needs expressed by the population before the onset of the crisis.

The constitutional reform qualitatively modified significant parts of the Cuban Constitution of 1976 besides those dealing with the concept of property. Among these were portions of the text about the political and social foundations of the state, the functioning of the local bodies of People's Power, the electoral system, and the legal status of religious believers and the lay character of the Cuban state. The reference to the dictatorship of the proletariat was struck from the Constitution; the role of the Communist Party was no longer to be the vanguard of the working class, but of the nation;[10] and the nongovernmental functions of the mass organizations were emphasized. Electoral mechanisms for the national and provincial representative bodies were made more direct. Finally, atheism ceased to be the official doctrine of the state.[11]

That these reforms in the constitutional text were not merely cosmetic is demonstrated by the legislation and policies of succeeding years. Besides the socioeconomic changes in the area of property relations, a new electoral law was passed and then implemented in the elections of December 1992, February 1993, and 1997–98.[12] Delegates to the National Assembly and to the provincial ones are now directly elected by district voters, in place of the previous system of indirect elections by the lower-level representative bodies. The commissions charged with selecting national and provincial candidates are directed by the trade unions and include other representative social organizations, in place of being directed by the Communist Party. The Communist Party may no longer intervene, as an organization, in this process. Although there is no electoral campaign, candidates meet with local voters and face their questioning. Once elected to provincial and national assemblies, the representatives are required to maintain regular contact with the voters—in contrast to the earlier system, in which only the delegates to the municipal assemblies held such periodic assemblies of "rendering account."

The nomination of district candidates by local assemblies, the absence of Communist Party directives to members about how to vote or whom to nominate, the universal, direct, and secret character of the suffrage, election by absolute majority at each level, election at specified periods—all of these traits add democracy to the process. Systematic implementation of this model in the midst of crisis presented a challenge to the socialist government, so that the results of 1992–93 and of 1997–98 took on the significance of a plebiscite.

Finally, the policy of affirming the lay character of the state and of eliminating discrimination against religious believers has continued to advance, culminating with the January 1998 visit of Pope John Paul II which offered the Catholic Church a major platform from which to speak on social, ideological, and political subjects with nearly unrestricted access to the population.

To what extent are all these changes meaningful for the political system?

The retention of a group of historic figures in the leadership of the government and state apparatus, and the presence of a single party with an unusual role (between state and civil society) are characteristic traits, but insufficient to represent the complexity of the Cuban system.[13] Several other factors are also essential to understanding its functioning and possible evolution: the particularity of the nation's historical process, including the revolution and the social and political order it brought; the nature of the consensus articulated in civil society; and the leadership's political style and its role in the reform process now under way.

Although preserving many of its structural characteristics, the political system has displayed increasing decentralization, flexibility, and pluralism. The key zones of popular participation have been strengthened, with a higher profile for civil society and its organic expressions, especially at the base.

The tendencies developing before and during the present crisis, without being conclusive, allow us to hypothesize the following possible dynamic for future years:[14]

- Maintenance of the single party, with a more and more fully democratic way of operating in its internal life, policies of more dynamic
interaction with the popular base (both members and nonmem-
bers), and greater diversity within its ranks

- Greater roles for the representative bodies of People's Power in political direction at all levels

- More diversification in the mass media, with the Party and state
maintaining control of the major organs parallel to a growth in
other media controlled by institutions, social organizations, and
other nongovernmental entities

- Continuing rationalization of the armed forces as part of the economic reform program, including increasing self-financing, at the
same time as these forces maintain the presence required by the
demands of national security and the preservation of stability for
peaceful development

- Greater presence and influence of the diverse sectors of Cuban society in the representative bodies of People's Power, including the
National Assembly

- Growth in the role and voice of unions in the country's life, including in the joint-venture sector of the economy

The challenges facing the political regime, as can be seen, cannot be
resolved by purely administrative measures nor by reducing politics to
speeches and mobilizations. In Cuba, as in any other country, the political sphere is greater than the sum of those spaces and mechanisms.
Understanding the nature of consensus is fundamental to understanding the course of politics in its multifaceted interaction with the society.
In new conditions, ideology spreads beyond the confines of official discourse into the context of social relations throughout the society. It does
not move under wraps; it expresses itself in the newly emerging social
relations, new codes, and distortions of the crisis. This ideological dynamic can be clearly seen in the way the effects of the crisis have eroded
consensus.

It is difficult to estimate the exact depth of this erosion because of the
critical conjuncture itself, which contributes to blurring how far it has

reached into the deepest structures of social psychology. In strictly political terms, there are no signs of rupture in the consensus nor of an emergent public consciousness in favor of breaking with the established order. But along with the natural expressions of unease and discontent that flare up in daily life, a new current of thinking is growing up, one that shows itself in debates that take place not only in public spaces and periodicals but also in political and social organizations and even in official institutions and bodies. To encourage such debate, facilitate it, and pay attention to it is part of a politics that responds to the new realities. The development of this debate is also affected by the difficulties of the whole process of internal change, in particular those created by the emergencies of daily life, the unpredictable supply of scarce basic resources (such as energy), and the concern for preserving the stability that implementing change requires.

The gradualist line taken by the reform process in Cuba has been recovering zones of consensus from the bewilderment provoked by the shock of the crisis. But this process does not evolve free of outside interference. The main such external factor is the nature of the relationship with the United States.

Domestic Impact of the Cuba-U.S. Conflict

The economic crisis and the end of the USSR sharpened a Cuban perception of national insecurity. This perception translated into a sense of exposure, vulnerability, and strategic imbalance in the face of a renewed threat that menaced not only the economic order or the political structure, but also the Cuban social system. National stability, domestic order, and international security are prioritized in Cuba.

This situation affects the political process and democratic paradigm in a variety of ways, which may be summarized as follows:

- The United States imposes punitive measures that restrict Cuba's freedom and self-determination, fundamental premises for any democratic functioning.

- The ongoing U.S. siege and the goal of intervening in the island's internal affairs contribute to maintaining a high level of precaution in relation to defense.

- The consequent mentality of a fortress under attack does not contribute to pluralism in Cuba.

- The crisis's narrowing of internal consensus exacerbates the perception of the threat to internal security that U.S. policies represent.

- The ideologization of the issue of democracy by the United States contrasts with the policies followed by other governments. Though other governments may criticize the Cuban political system, such criticisms are not translated into conditions for sustaining relations with the island.

The U.S. policy of pressure has made it easier for those resistant to internal changes to appeal to the argument that any policies which might be viewed as concessions to the United States will weaken Cuban positions. These factors also provoke a sort of allergic reaction within Cuban political and ideological discourse to such concepts as market, human rights, pluralism, civil society, and transition. This reaction can be explained not only by today's particular sense of insecurity but also by the ideological residue left by the U.S.-Cuban conflict over a span of nearly forty years.

The basic issue in the U.S. confrontation with Cuba remains the same: the nature of the Cuban political system and the American goal of bringing about a fundamental change. Thus, in spite of changes in the international system and the absence of a domestic or regional political crisis, relations between the two countries remain unstable. This instability is aggravated by several factors: the absence of international security structures between Cuba and the United States; the lack of accords that would oblige both states to act against violations of international law (for instance, the hijacking of ships or the violation of each other's airspace); the prevailing political climate in the Cuban community enclaves in the United States, which has blocked strict application of U.S. law and limited the independence of the court system to act against such crimes as the organization of terrorist activities; the volatility of the Northamerican political atmosphere with respect to Cuba; and therefore the domestic contamination of any new possibilities between the two countries.

The main progress in bilateral relations has come in the "traditional" area of migration, which also has a domestic dimension for the United States. The negotiation of emigration/immigration accords in September 1994 and May 1995, as well as their subsequent application and the continuing bilateral talks on this issue, have produced some significant results. In particular, the accords have drastically reduced the flow of undocumented emigrants who risk their safety crossing the Straits of Florida or Guantanamo Bay in the hope of being rescued by the U.S. Coast Guard or Navy. The agreements have also placed undocumented Cubans attempting to enter the United States on a more equal basis with those coming from other countries of the Caribbean and Latin America. In fact, the United States has recognized that the motives of the majority of the Cuban emigrants are economic or related to family reunification. Finally, the accords have established the obligation of both countries' coast guard forces to cooperate in search-and-rescue operations and the return of boats to Cuban territory.

Other areas in which Cuba and United States could cooperate, if there were a political will to do so, would be prevention of air and sea hijacking and the fight against drug traffickers.

Cuban national security policy has indicated a disposition toward regional multilateral cooperation in areas of mutual trust, and in other aspects that could benefit not only the two countries but also their international environment, especially in the Caribbean.

The epitome of the obstacles built up over the course of nine U.S. administrations is represented by the Helms-Burton Act, which tends to freeze the two countries' relations in the limbo of the Cold War. With respect to Cuba's internal processes, its logic is counterproductive. The changes taking place in the island's society, economy, and politics must do so against the tide of bilateral tensions.

In general, not only in terms of relations with the United States, Cuba's foreign relations are important to its internal dynamic.

Foreign Affairs in Domestic Politics

In the new international system of the post–Cold War era, Cuban foreign policy priorities have gone through important changes, as have the means available to carry them out. The peace negotiations in southwestern Africa and in Central America, the end of the Comecon, and finally the dismantling of the USSR and the European socialist camp transformed the magnetic field of Cuban policy in the global context. Along with their above-discussed negative effects in the domestic sphere, these events—not exclusively associated with the end of the East-West polarity, but also with regional dynamics—demanded that Cuba reexamine its available means and achievable goals.

One of the consequences of this transition process in the island's foreign relations has been the increased importance of diplomacy and participation in multilateral bodies at both the regional and the global level.

Renewed activism on the part of Cuban diplomacy is expressed in such areas as international cooperation, where important strides have been taken in recent years. Cuba's policy has sought to consolidate prioritized lines of development, establish mechanisms such as free trade zones, and secure technical assistance for new sectors such as the UBPCs. The efforts at international cooperation, nevertheless, are unlikely to imply acceptance of schemes that would outline new political models, overall development models, or privatization formulas.

As for nongovernmental organizations, Cuba now maintains relations with more than 170 NGOs in forty-two countries.[15] The majority (around 90 percent) of the contributions from such NGOs have a domestic effect, because they fall under the rubric of "aid and assistance."[16] An estimated fifty Cuban NGOs are benefiting from international cooperation in sustainable development projects.[17] If still modest in absolute terms, the role of foreign NGOs has grown and may be tending to consolidate, although the organizations' presence appears to remain concentrated in the areas affected by the crisis. The foreign NGOs that have acted without directly or indirectly attempting to place conditions on their aid seem to have a more stable position.

In terms of Cuban policies toward Latin America, the multilateral mechanisms that hold the most strategic interest are two: the Ibero-American summits and the Association of Caribbean States (ACS). The prospect of a Havana summit in 1999 represents an important access point for Cuba's process of encounter and reinsertion in the heart of that first community. The ACS, for its part, is the most important regional organization in which the island participates.[18]

In conformity with the agreements reached at the ACS summit of 1995 with respect to commerce, tourism, and transportation, Cuba has

broadened air and sea contact with the subregion, has fostered cooperation in the tourist field, and in general has explored the strengthening of
commercial ties. The possibilities of cooperation in areas such as environment and culture, and of beginning common efforts against drug
trafficking in the Basin, have been discussed.

From this point of view, Cuba's process of regional reinsertion will not
necessarily take place through the classic Pan-American channels such
as the OAS but rather (if in contradictory and gradual ways) through
multiple routes where realism and mutual interests, both national and
subregional, prevail.

In contrast to the situation prevailing between Cuba and the United
States, the liberalization of trade and investment at the continental level
may play a central role in this reinsertion. Cooperation with other countries in the region supports the opening up of Cuba's economy, its growing trade with the region, and the advance of its economic reform.

The U.S. embargo notwithstanding, the process of reinsertion is being pushed along by trade and investment liberalization at the regional
level, and also by Cuban government policies promoting association between Cuban and foreign enterprises, exploitation of complementarities
(as with energy-exporting countries that have a demand for Cuban products), joint development of tourism, and application of flexible mechanisms for resolving the Cuban debt.

The embargo nonetheless impedes Cuba's access to its main natural
market and the international financial system, and limits its connections
with the hemispheric trade liberalization process. If the embargo were to
be lifted, the eventual presence of the United States in the Cuban
economy would have a considerable impact on its internal and external
dynamic. This would not necessarily change the predominant tendency
toward a diversified reinsertion in the hemisphere.

The Cuban system does not match the political model in force in
many countries of the region. Nonetheless, businessmen, churches,
nongovernmental organizations, and important political figures have declared themselves in favor of the island's reintegration into the hemisphere, and in favor of lifting the measures that seek to isolate it. As
Hugo Azcuy has pointed out, foreign questioning of Cuba on human
rights grounds is not so much concerned with the legal guarantees or
degree of democracy in its system as with the nature of the political sys-

tem itself.[19] The Cuban government therefore perceives a perpetual intervention in its internal affairs, an attempt to create a moral and legal situation that forces it to make political concessions. For this reason, it is very unlikely that the island could find fully satisfying ways of working with regional political bodies on that subject—although it is clear that Cuba would prefer dialogue to the isolation promoted by the United States.

The Cuban government disagrees with the use of mechanisms and structures of compulsion for the establishment of liberal democracies in the region, especially when these imply more or less open forms of interventionism. From a Cuban point of view, imposing a given model of democracy contradicts the acceptance of a pluralist political context which a genuinely democratic inter-American system would require. As Juan Valdés Paz has argued, what political democracy implies to the Cuban government is national independence, the defense of the rights of all its citizens, equality, and popular participation in political and economic power. From this perspective, popular democracy in Cuba must be strengthened in accord with circumstances and without risking the independence and security of the country and the revolution. In any case, the political system has evolved in uninterrupted fashion toward a state of law: legitimizing its restrictions through specific juridical norms on the one hand, and subordinating its behavior to a legally constituted order on the other.[20]

The logic of hemispheric foreign relations, the neoliberal current itself, the opportunity offered by the Cuban policy of opening to foreign investment and international commerce—all these produce a marginal effect that leads toward communication between the island and the rest of the hemisphere. In relation to issues such as economic integration, free trade, sustainable development, and conservation of the natural environment—as well as cooperation in energy, strengthening telecommunications, and cooperation in science, technology, and tourism—an inter-American logic would favor increased interchange with Cuba. At the same time, those trying to address the problems of eradicating poverty and discrimination, and in particular improving education and public health and strengthening the role of women, can make use of the lessons and merits of the Cuban experience.[21]

Final Considerations

It is difficult to close without discussing certain features of most models of transition presented by parties outside Cuba for the island's future. First, there is a strange tendency to view "transition" as something excluding the actual political actors and social subjects of Cuban society today. Second, these models are put forward by institutions and figures that are themselves distant from Cuban reality and the Cuban political system, and that enjoy, to a very striking extent, the sponsorship of the U.S. government or agencies dependent upon it.

Independently of what might be desirable regarding reconciliation between Cuban politics and the politics of the exiles, the distance between the parties is sufficiently great to make an understanding most improbable. Taking into account the state of relations between Cuba and the United States, and especially the Helms-Burton Act, this possibility grows even more remote. The legal standing that this U.S. law offers to Cuban exiles whose properties were nationalized adds to the acrimony between old and new proprietors.

The possible transition, in contrast, is one led and controlled by the Cuban government itself, the institutions of the state and civil society, with the participation of important social actors old and new. The pace and the cost of this process depend on the participants' capacity to cooperate and find common ground in the midst of a complex and often adverse domestic and foreign context. In any case, the process of reform and political change is already under way. In the end, it will have to lead to a socialist society different from the one that has existed on the island until the present.

7

On Discourse

"The question is," said Alice, "whether you *can* make words mean
so many different things."

"The question is," said Humpty Dumpty, "which is to be master—
that's all."

—**Lewis Carroll**, *Through the Looking Glass*

Alice's dialogue with Humpty Dumpty unfolds as part of a disquisition
on language. The Egg expects to be able to use words as he pleases, because he sees them as his paid employees (even if some are more resistant to his will than others). Alice, with her stubborn streak of common
sense, is confused by such a capricious manner of assigning new meanings. For Humpty, a philosopher of realpolitik, power is the key to semantics.

Beneath the supposedly subjective land of language, Carroll seems to
be telling us, lie power relations underground. However anarchic the
semantic fields of many words, they are held together by a logic that reflects social relations. The apparently arbitrary frame of discourse may
be read in relation to a given social order of things.

According to the definition commonly accepted by linguists and soci-
ologists, discourse consists of "actual instances of everyday communication: a conversation between friends, a classroom interaction, a newspaper editorial."[1] Discourses cannot be reduced to mere filters or prisms
through which we see real society, nor, of course, are they its simple reflection. Rather they are an integral part of the social whole and its contradictions. How could they not be, since they constitute its basic system
of communication? As Adam Schaff points out, the categories and grammatical structure offered by a given language lend themselves to a particular form of *perception* of reality; only as the language changes may

perceptions change too. Hence the centrality of language as a symbolic and signifying system affecting cultural development.[2] A critique of a way of using language, therefore, leads to a critique of the social relations of which that discourse forms a part.

Language and Society

Studying the relations between language and society requires paying attention to the ways in which expressions serve as a medium of action and interpretation, a means through which history is produced and society reproduced. The issue is to understand the sociohistorical conditions in which a given language establishes its legitimacy and is acquired by some people and imposed on others as the dominant form in use.[3]

These relations are established and represented at the level of speech. The linguist Carlos Paz, in referring to so-called vulgar uses of language, points out that patterns of conduct are hidden behind the words of daily speech. These words have been created or imbued with semantic content and stylistic and sociolinguistic values. So, in rejecting "vulgarities," says Paz, we reject not only words but patterns of social conduct. Nonetheless, he adds, social norms about what constitutes acceptable language stem not only from social stratification but also from the hierarchy of appropriate situations within a given social class; he reminds us that "popular speech is the patrimony of people of varied origins, and popular terms and turns of phrase flow from the most illiterate as well as the most cultivated tongues."[4]

In practice, in Cuba, it is not always possible to draw boundaries that would show given linguistic modes—vocabulary, syntax, oral "grammars," root words, reservoirs of meaning—being used exclusively by certain groups or differing radically from group to group. The porousness of these boundaries also has a transnational, or global, dimension. Simultaneous reinforcement of heterogeneity in the social structure and growing homogeneity in discourse and ways of thinking are characteristic of the process of globalization.[5]

Everyday speech is the factory in which new codes of reality are built. In Cuba, the adoption of colloquial terms such as *shopping* or *paladares,* the identification of social types such as *jineteras* or *macetas,* the coining of expressions like "escaping," "stub out the cigar," and "getting away with"—all articulate the consciousness of a new global referent.[6] Such linguistic mediation of reality is a richer phenomenon than the mere incorporation of foreign terms for consumer goods, like the neologisms *videocasetera* or *nintendo*. Rather, it is a process of knowledge creation that includes both a given social relationship and the speaker's attitude toward that relationship. In this process, social subjects create or adopt expressions that take account of the phenomena making themselves felt in daily life experience, phenomena toward which the subjects (the speakers) need to orient and locate themselves in a practical way.

Terms that belong to an established order, that have now been worn out by use, cede ground to other terms—either new ones or terms that have been out of use for some time. In the process, the "new" language articulates a new subjectivity.

Naturally, this phenomenology of discourse cannot be mechanically put to use as an observatory from which to view the class struggle. We are dealing with a much subtler process, one subject to many influences. For example, it is true that the once universal term *compañero/a* has been losing ground to a variety of other appellations, the most conspicuous of which is *señor/a*. This displacement is occurring not only in the world of *paladares* and private parking lots, of *shoppings* and tourist hotels, but in broader and broader contexts. This substitution could be interpreted as one more epiphenomenon of the crisis; that is, as an indicator of ideological change and a reflection of a new sense of values. However, the popularization of *señor/a* in given circumstances could also be attributed to a process of wearing out or emptying of the original subjective meaning of *compañero/a*, a process of semantic degradation thanks to *compañero/a*'s overuse in everyday discourse, in which the word lost its meaning in terms of a person's identity and became merely a formal term of address. In that second interpretation, the substitution would reflect a revaluation of discourse at the level of interpersonal relations. To restore the original dignity of *señor/a*, previously devalued, and to reject the generic use of *compañero/a* by using it in a more discriminating fashion, could have the effect of restoring to the latter its proper meaning of shared identity.

Still, either of those hypotheses (which are not, by the way, mutually exclusive) would have to deal with a discourse that is changing in the context of changed social relations. Certain terms' falling out of use is not the only sign of this alteration. The crisis, too, is only one of its expressions. The crisis might be defined as the destructuring of an economic, social, and discursive order that is no longer what it once was, yet has not evolved into something completely new. This process is not limited to the sphere of politics or the realm of institutions such as the workplace, the school, and the mass media. The fact that it is occurring in such a literate society as Cuba's confers a multiplier effect. The modification of what classic linguistics would call "the relation between the signifier and the signified" has a much greater reach.

A Literate *Polis*

In the workbook that Literacy Campaign volunteers used in 1961, the first lesson was devoted to vowels; it included an explanation of the Organization of American States, whose Spanish initials are OEA. The fact that an urban adolescent like myself became the teacher of the head of a peasant family in the mountains was part of what a certain jargon would call the "transgression of sociolinguistic stratification." This transgression was possible only by means of a tremendous act of political and social engineering. The proposition that *this* teacher would explain to *that* student not only the Spanish vowels but the significance of the OAS was an ambitious one in that neither of the two actors was prepared to understand the OAS. Yet it had a deep symbolic meaning. The phrases of a shared political discourse created a shared referent, regardless of how difficult or remote its meaning may have been. The common referent helped to legitimize that student-teacher situation, and later to legitimize the transgression of all sorts of stratifications with the founding of a new and better educational system.

The establishment of the new system, in turn, fulfilled a still greater civil purpose: transformation of the society. In the terminology of José Martí, this was "freeing the serf from his ignorance." The written language and all that accompanies it became part of the set of values shared by all the members of Cuban society. Discourses were no longer confined to separate and sealed compartments. Poor people, ordinary people, appropriated the realms of language from which they had been barred, and made them part of their culture. In the new order, knowledge became a central element in social prestige. The children of peasants who learned to read and write in the Literacy Campaign could dream of becoming (among other things) teachers and authors.

The spread of language within popular culture transformed the culture's codes. Literacy teachers and literacy students—and millions more citizens with them—shared and reshaped a Spanish that spilled beyond the boundaries of the standard dictionaries. Even for high culture, the standard was no longer that of the Royal Academy of the Spanish Language and its friends. We might say that language, too, freed itself from the structures of control.

As part of this process, discourse acquired new twists, new terms, new tropes that reflected values, beliefs, ideals, and aspirations appropriate to an ideology of liberation that became dominant. The preeminence of this ideology did not lie in any preestablished order—in a given mode of organizing the economy, of planning development, channeling citizen participation, or structuring the political system. The values embedded in the new discourse (which was rapidly becoming a social fact) were more than the image of a given superstructure. This social discourse, deeply implanted in conscience and consciousness, took shape in the context of a new political culture.

The match between social discourse and attitudes, on the one hand, and the underlying political culture, on the other, explains the effectiveness of the process of communication—for instance, between literacy teacher and student—including the relative ease with which completely foreign cultural patterns were assimilated.

Among the Literacy Campaign workers, the latest fashion in foreign languages was Russian. The borrowing of Russian words for use in slang expressions and even in student conga lines came long before the decade of the 1970s and had nothing to do with that later sovietization. Naturally, the cultural empathy would have been unthinkable if things Russian had not come into vogue for political reasons. But the popular taste for Russian survived even such vicissitudes as the 1962 missile crisis (and the student conga lines that publically insulted the leaders of the Soviet Union at that time). Russian was popular because it symbolized the "other" language, the language of socialism, which Cuba had culturally adopted and imagined as a world project capable of opposing the political and cultural order of imperialism.

To a certain extent, later history brought with it a dichotomy of opposing paradigms symbolized in the language sphere by Russian and English. The badge of language came to help or hinder the importation of cultural products both good and bad. The privileging of Russian, for instance, meant that citing Russian sources would testify to the seriousness of a scholarly work, even if the subject of the work was Mayan civilization and the Russian author cited was a complete unknown. Citations of Anglo-Saxon sources were often less convincing, even in the case of an author affiliated with Marxist currents and writing about his or her own national culture.

Naturally, this norm was subject to a variety of interpretations, some more monolithic than others, and therefore to more or less strict measures of possible deviation. Depending on how strict this measure was, some observers could see signs of opposition where others saw signs of something in common; certain alien fashions could be rejected as perversions or adopted as acceptable patterns, and so on. But these interpretations of the norm, which spread widely through Cuban society, were contained within fairly well established limits. In general, deviations from the prevailing canons consigned their holders to a marginalized position.

Within this relative homogeneity, education played a central role. In a literate *polis*, to speak and write up to academic standards, and to read as a practice of daily life, were socially well regarded. These capacities were considered signs of prestige, personal merit, and civic potential. To be an administrator, an agricultural engineer, or a professional political cadre was perfectly compatible with browsing in bookstores, sounding off about a newly published anthology of Northamerican short stories, or offering interpretations of the lyrics of the New Song movement. Similarly, to be interested in philosophy or culture did not lead to being stereotyped as ignorant of concrete realities, uninterested in the daily newspaper, or unlikely to amount to much.

Within this framework of communication, the discourse of personal progress was not constructed around the idea of *winning* but of *self-improvement*. The signs of progress were not necessarily the material trappings of power but rather, above all, social recognition. Characteristic linguistic codes did develop and did generate certain formulas in speech and writing, but these codes were expansive and able to assimilate new developments. They did not adopt a final shape, nor did they close the universe of discourse. They tended to generate rules, but the rules were neither universal nor invulnerable; they won out only temporarily or in certain circles. For instance, the controversy over the use of *malas palabras* (swearwords), though a distant curiosity when viewed from the present, reached a fever pitch more than once; this suggests that it was about something less obvious than the correction of inferior speech.[7] Today, when characters on popular television programs parade their well-developed street vocabularies, disquisitions on artistic uses of language are not concerned with "correcting" such dialogue—although they still may carry some baggage that goes beyond questions of grammar.

Politics of Language

In book 4 of *Gargantua and Pantagruel,* Rabelais sends his characters sailing through a frigid ocean filled with frozen words of many colors and textures. When the words melt, they pronounce themselves. "Don't forget that here the words have not thawed," Pantagruel warns as he tosses handfuls of "sharp and bloody" words on the deck. When his fellow travelers can't understand the meaning of these sounds, he explains that they "belong to a barbarian language."[8]

If we pass over Rabelais's carnivalesque world and Grand Guignol tone, we find that his image of frozen words is not so far removed from discourse phenomena we can observe today. That is, as living beings his words are independent of consciousness (as a philosophy text might say) and have intrinsic qualities of their own. Today, words like "market" or "democracy," "civil society" or "transition" display a certain degree of that frozen state. Each one alludes to a global referent that is homogeneous but serves to differentiate. Whatever the critical examination they may deserve as concepts, these terms are frozen into a state that has little to do with their original meaning. They are signifiers in a "barbarian discourse" in the sense of a discourse that comes from afar. As such, they cannot be understood; they need to be thawed. To put it another way, they must be extracted from the global discourse and restored, critically, to their original significance. In that way they can be used in a fuller and more effective fashion, and not only applied to phenomena outside Cuba.

"Sharp and bloody" expressions also abound. Puns, double entendres, and other inventions of popular speech—what are they if not subversions of a solemn discursive order? I do not mean to propose an exaggerated relationship between the diverse forms of verbal transgressions so abundant in popular speech and the expression of disruptions in ideologically dominant values or patterns. The issue I am raising here is, rather, the convergence of certain attitudes about language and certain ways of conceiving values and ideas as ritually prescribed forms.

"Politically correct" discourse (a curious term which leaps across ideological barriers) tends to be accompanied by a fixed lexicon, semantics, and even syntax. These codes are unwritten but strictly differentiable, and their norms can be as inflexible as the rules of grammar. The use of terms from outside the code produces the same kind of automatic negative reflex as an error in spelling or punctuation. This reaction cannot necessarily be reduced to an ideological or political rationale; at base, it consists of a cultural predisposition to see the norm as a countersign, an indication that one is traveling through safe and well-known terrain. By contrast, the deviation will surely lead to someplace unexplored, foreign, unsafe, wrong; therefore it is suspect and untrustworthy.

In parallel fashion, what we might call the "public sphere" of language includes modes that, while not necessarily oppositional, are at the margin of the "grammatical" order. Though the relationship of language, political culture, and ideology may be very subtle, it can also be made explicit. This occurs, for instance, with some popular jokes.

The role of the political joke and its function as a mirror of the contradictions within socialism in Eastern Europe—as Abel Prieto has pointed out in his study *El humor de Misha*—may be considered paradigmatic.[9] This genre, so popular in Cuban culture of all periods, offers a sort of prism through which the most varied shades of collective conscious are refracted. The joke, tour de force of oral language, is a fine barometer that registers changes in the psychological climate of a society (civil society and political society too). Much more effectively than many opinion polls, the joke captures the intimate heartbeat of public opinion. It narrates a story of national political history, creates mythological heroes and antiheroes, and exorcizes discourses of all sorts. The genre par excellence of popular speech and gesticulation, it becomes a thesaurus of formulae, turns of phrases, maxims, and off-color or off-center sayings. In this collective laboratory, instantaneous codes of social communication are constantly re-created.

Given all the foregoing, it is hard to ignore the preeminence of language in its specific condition as a carrier of ideas for both ideological and political ends. This is especially true in a moment of crisis. In fact, we must recognize the need for not just one language but several. Such an acceptance of diversity—of existing discourses and possible languages—is grounded in the need for effective ideological action that succeeds in its mission to convince, rather than action that is schematic, overly generalized, and dogmatic.[10]

If effective ideological action requires the use of a variety of persuasive, nondogmatic discursive modes, it could be useful to first characterize dogmatic discourse in its various forms and mutations. Can we recognize its imprint in certain linguistic modes, certain ways of speaking or writing? As the British economist Joan Robinson says, we can recognize a hippopotamus even if we can't formulate an exact definition. Dogmatic discourse, just as clearly as a hippopotamus, has its distinctive features. These could be the object of systematic and detailed study, perhaps with the instruments of linguistics and semiotics. But in any case, we can perceive dogma as a kind of basic cultural attitude, shaped and reinforced by other pedagogies.

Before the globalization so much talked about today, our insertion in the former socialist international system left us a heritage that affected language codes, mentalities, and prevailing visions. For instance, if we open the *Brief Political Dictionary* of L. Onikov and N. Shishlin to the letter *S*, we find that "Sectarianism is an anti-Marxist, opportunist, leftist current in the revolutionary workers' movement, characterized by its scorn for the role of labor unions." And "The ideological forms of political sectarianism are dogmatism, talmudism, and a denial of the need for development of Marxism-Leninism within the changing historical situation, the exclusion of parliamentary forms of struggle, etc."[11] This astounding definition should be enough to illustrate to what extent a compendium of vocabulary and correct usage can contribute to a kind of cultural conditioning that favors a certain way of reasoning. This "barbarian" influence (from the East, not the West) extended far beyond the placid precincts of dictionaries.

Alongside the noteworthy accomplishments of those societies, their Wall was more than a geopolitical artifact. It became part of a type of discourse. The idea of a walled-in culture, constructed out of words like stones from a quarry, symbolically expressed the weakness of that formidable fortress.[12]

This linguistic and artistic influence wore out over time. It is well known that among the younger Cuban generations the popularity of the Russian language and other aspects of Eastern European culture had declined long before perestroika and the end of the USSR. Attempts to graft socialist realism onto Cuban art also failed to flower, though not for lack of determined (and sometimes distinguished) gardeners, especially in some epochs and at certain levels of the teaching of literature and art. This long exposure bore more fruit in the realm of mentalities than in foreign language preferences and artistic creation. Undeniably, its influence is most visible in ideological discourse and training.

Ideological discourse, it is well worth pointing out, is just one of many discourses that coexist horizontally. The notion of a predominant ideological discourse does not exclude other "nonideological" discourses—aesthetic, religious, sexual—as widespread and dominant as a given constellation of specifically ideological values. Thus, however predominant an ideology may be, it does not subsume those other contents of the prevailing culture of a given period; rather there is a reciprocal relationship like that of the fluids in communicating vessels in physics. To ignore those other, alternative cultural discourses—or to administratively suppress or amputate them in the name of public health—may have a short-term effect, but historically it has not proved to be effective in the long run.

At the same time, a discourse that has descended into stereotype does not recover its political power the way a factory may be renewed by replacing obsolete technologies with up-to-date ones. The extent to which a discourse has lost its strength does not have so much to do with the modernity of its media of communications, or with the political camp it is associated with. If, as asserted above, the discourses that populate real life represent concrete and contradictory social relations, a discourse will prevail according to its capacity to be *real*. In other words, according to its capacity to make these social relations explicit, to dialogue with the other discourses in circulation, to summon them and lead them, to interact with them and contaminate their codes.

A stereotyped discourse is caught on the horns of a dilemma. Either it must undergo a profound transformation, or else it will go on reproducing itself as before, condemned to lose its way, fall out of daily use and be ignored or abandoned because it has ceased to communicate (that is, it has decayed to the point that it no longer works). The space it has occupied will not remain empty, because other discourses, new or revived, will bring their communicative force to bear and begin to displace it in practice.

A close examination of these other discourses active within our current society may reveal their nuances, their diversity, their confusion, and their imports from abroad. Like other phenomena in the economy, ideology, culture, social psychology, and individual behavior, the nature of language and its discursive manifestations are not decided from some point in the superstructure. Rather, they obey strong dynamics within social relations. The essence of socialist culture—of values, aspirations, and ideals—is reproduced on the level of day-to-day relationships. That is where the real factory of ideology hums.

To intervene effectively in that dynamic with a specific discourse, in the context of a literate *polis,* is a much more complex operation than the social engineering of the Literacy Campaign. At a minimum, it requires the capacity to do three things: to reflect the multiplicity and differentiation of the social body, to communicate very effectively, and to minimize the degree of antagonism to other cultural discourses. This activity must take place in the fundamental sphere of real society, where everyday modes of thinking and acting are born, die, and reappear, along with the words that identify them.

s the oxymoron of three Cubans who *don't* talk been adopted so
tioningly by so many?

Society Mute?

ociety in general tends to be identified with the spaces of public
zation where codes and values are transmitted, cultural habits and
s of conduct are formed, ideological interaction takes place, and a
type of social relations is reproduced. What Gramsci called "pri-
pparatus of hegemony" takes charge of this: the schools, labor and
organizations, books and periodicals, churches, and the like. Yet in
se of a socialist society like Cuba, many of these organizations are
not in the private but in the state sector. This situation has led
observers—especially those who still confuse civil society with free
prise—to jump to the conclusion that those organizations are noth-
t tentacles of the state bureaucracy, divorced from civil society. The
for those given to such thinking is that in a socialist society like
, the universities, professional and religious associations, commu-
nd labor organizations, and cultural and academic publications are
spaces of civil society where the cultural and ideological variables in
quation of hegemony are daily reproduced.

his dynamic of civil society emerged as a subject of discussion in the
conditions brought on in Cuba by the transition and crisis of the
os. In these circumstances, the production of ideology is not limited
iscussions within the established political discourse; rather, it over-
vs into the area of social relations. Ideological conflict emerges from
contradictions generated by phenomena such as growing inequality;
presence of enclaves, styles, and ways of life characteristic of capital-
t; the distortions of dollarization; the social impact of tourism; and the
earance of new patterns of speech and codes of conduct. In this con-
t, a relative shrinkage of the consensus that existed before the crisis
y be seen. It would be difficult to measure that shrinkage exactly, be-
use the rigors of the crisis cloud any estimation of what has changed in
e deepest structures of social psychology. If the question being asked is
out political stability, however, no signs of a fundamental crack in the
nsensus are evident, such as would be the case if a citizens' conscious-
ess favoring replacement of the political system had emerged. What

Three Cubans Talk

Political Culture, Ideological Debate

> Truth cannot penetrate a (
> —**Borges, "El Aleph"**

Three Cubans are standing on a corner tall
what they're doing is arguing. Their opinion
the whole gamut of the game from the deb
Industriales on a hard chopper to short in the
controversial strategy employed in selecting tl
the miniseries with Japan. Nothing in the gan
Cubans take up anything that can affect it in
exception but the rule. But could anyone supp
their tongues puts their loyalty in question? A
issue ought to see the three of them in action,
country, the afternoon that Cuba is playing the
course, the value that triumphs above all is pure
point where our three Cubans may be applaudin,
has put up a line score of no runs, no hits, and s
That's called good sportsmanship. Or as Pierre c
noblesse oblige.

This image raises two questions that have in
time. Number one: Doesn't this baseball culture, v
an intense participant, the game a widespread pul
mond a fertile and democratic space of controver
and power of the Cuban game at the internationa

Why ha
unques

Is Civil

Civil s
sociali
patter
certai
vate a
social
the ca
found
some
enter
ing b
news
Cuba
nity
also
the

new
199
to d
flo
the
the
isr
ap
te
m
ca
th
al
c
n

can be seen are tendencies that anticipate changes in the way the system functions.

Along with such tendencies that are reconstructive of consensus—in favor of change but not of negating the ideological underpinnings of socialism—other and opposite political conceptions have also developed, especially at the individual level. Attitudes that could be identified as foreign to socialism—that is, contradictory not only to the current system but to the values of any more democratic socialism that might be possible in Cuba—can be observed daily. Although not expressed in an articulated matter in the current conditions, they should not be underestimated. These attitudes are not characterized by *dissenting* from particular policies being carried out; rather, they are *dissident* from the socialist underpinnings.[1] Those who *dissent* in Cuba exercise a fundamental right, that of being able to criticize socialist policies from within that same camp. On the other hand, those who are dissident deny their own former convictions, abandoning an ideal they no longer share in either doctrinal or practical terms. They don't want to change the system, they want to liquidate it and replace it with the *other one*.

If these tendencies evident in daily life tend to be underestimated in Cuba, outside the island just the opposite tends to occur: they are overestimated, and moreover they are confused with the so-called human rights groups, whose domestic political irrelevance (in terms of the expression of consensus) is matched only by the inordinate publicity they receive outside.

In parallel fashion, intellectual and cultural circles have been generating a new outlook that anticipates a new socialist political culture, of which early signs may be seen not only in the debates that take place in public spaces and periodicals but in social organizations and even in public institutions such as universities and in government departments. To facilitate this debate, to extend and take advantage of it, is a political necessity that grows out of the new realities. Its development, nonetheless, is affected by the difficulties of the internal political process—in particular those created by the rigors of daily life and by that special domestic circumstance associated with the constant U.S. pressure.

One among many examples of the renewal of Cuban thought can be found in the spectrum of periodicals. The gradual recovery from the Special Period has seen the emergence, or reemergence, of more journals giving voice to currents of cultural, social, and political thought than ever before. *La Gaceta de Cuba, Temas, Contracorriente, Debates Americanos, Opus Habana, Marx Ahora, Caminos, Cultura y Desarrollo, Del Caribe, Casa de las Américas, Revista de Ciencias Sociales, Revolución y Cultura, Unión, Cuba Socialista, Islas,* and more, including various publications of religious institutions, reflect what may be considered a period of debate, revival, and diversification in the terrain of ideas.

Many of these publications are not organs of any given institution. Even when they are, they tend to offer space in their pages to a diverse collection of perspectives and themes that do not reflect an institutional point of view. Most of them thus form, in fact, organs of Cuban civil society, indispensable for following the development of new thinking, the intellectual movement, and the discussion of ideas on the island. Among the numerous recurrent topics they cover, all subjects of current controversy, are: civil society, critical revision of the history of Cuba and of Marxism, gender issues, the consciousness of Cuban youth, race relations and racial prejudice, the rise of religion, the culture of Cubans abroad, fiction, theater, and visual arts as spaces for confrontation of ideas, the crisis of values, the role of the mass media, growing social diversity and inequality, and reevaluation of the prerevolutionary republic.

Although they do not always appear cited as principal sources in books published outside Cuba about the topics taken up in their pages, these magazines are read on the island not only within cultural and academic circles but in political ones as well. They are also read in technological institutes and teachers' colleges, high schools, military academies, public libraries, schools for political cadres, religious seminaries, and government departments, and among ordinary citizens too. The source of all this interest resides in the fact that these publications articulate in intellectually structured form a wide debate not only within the fields of art, literature, and social thought but also in the other dimensions of culture that affect society, ideology, and politics. The contemporary and polemical character of their approaches offers a new opportunity for reflection.

In contrast to the oft-presented image of a binary Cuba apparently inhabited only by Fidel and the "dissident groups," an island whose thinking population have all taken up residence abroad, attention to this debate and the movement of ideas that accompanies it could contribute to a representation closer to reality, beyond the discourses officially accepted in other latitudes.

Political Debate or Monologue?

To what extent has a culture of debate consolidated itself in Cuba? To what degree has it spread beyond academic circles and cultural publications?

There exists an established culture that has incorporated the defense of the Cuban identity and nation and the affirmation of its ideological principles of sovereignty, independence, social justice, and social development. There is also a recognized need for interchange of ideas, discussion of internal problems, and implementation of organic and participatory mechanisms that will lead to "concrete" solutions. There is a declared need for informative communication with the exterior, specialized treatment of certain topics, and mastery of skills that facilitate the country's reinsertion in the international sphere. But a debate over ideas implies a larger horizon than that.

In the past ten years, outside academic circles and cultural publications, thorny topics previously isolated or ignored have been publicly discussed: religious, racial, or sexual discrimination, problems associated with corruption and with dollarization, environmental damage both urban and rural, prostitution and other deviant behavior resulting from the growth of tourism, the presence of marginality, crime, the impact of the crisis on vulnerable sectors such as the elderly and low-income, and the ineffectiveness of some mechanisms of participation.

Not only the social sciences but also Cuban literature, visual arts, theater, and cinema have explored these problems in depth. The defiant works of some authors who were regarded in their moment as dissidents, or of the latter-day exiles of the Special Period, now pale beside works winning prizes in Cuba even in contests organized by "official institutions." As an example, consider the stories and novels written and published in Cuba since the 1990s by young authors (Alberto Garrido, Ronaldo Menéndez, Mylene Fernández, José Manuel Prieto, Eduardo del Llano) and by the not-so-young (Arturo Arango, Leonardo Padura, Guillermo Vidal, Miguel Mejides, Abel Prieto, Mirta Yáñez, Francisco

López Sacha), or consider the works of well-known playwrights (Alberto Pedro, Abilio Estévez, Reynaldo Montero) which are staged today in the major theaters of the island by prestigious directors (Carlos Celdrán, Flora Lauten, Carlos Díaz), or the cinema of directors honored in the film festivals of Havana (Fernando Pérez, Juan Carlos Tabío, Arturo Sotto). The main themes of many of these works would have been unmentionable in a supposed totalitarian political and cultural climate: the impact of the debacle of socialism, the heartrending experiences of the Angolan war and of the rafters, the recurrent presence of prostitution, drugs, and other evidence of a revived underworld; so would previously taboo subjects such as homosexuality. Beyond this wave of issues that infused the works of the late nineties, contemporary Cuban literature and art have carried out a profound investigation of what is happening to the society's values and of the pitfalls of daily life.

Hence, what is under thorough review today is the very foundations—and meaning—of socialism as a social order and culture in Cuba.

Not only writers and artists, periodicals, experts and researchers have participated in this debate that emerges from civil society or is promoted by groups within it. Community leaders, elected local legislators, churches and religious figures, professional associations, NGOs, political leaders, environmentalists, state officials, and ordinary citizens are also involved.

The breadth and pluralism of this debate have expanded notably. Nonetheless, limitations of various sorts persist. The limitations are related to the effective use of research in the enrichment of the debate; difficulty in acquiring information and data on some social problems, or in discussing sensitive aspects of these (explained by the argument that they are susceptible to being politically manipulated); the minor presence of this discussion in the mass media; and the bureaucratic compartmentalization of certain topics of public interest. There also persist—and these are no less important—cultural and psychosocial predispositions within civil society itself that do not always facilitate the culture of dialogue or the richness of the exchange.

At the same time, international factors have had contradictory effects on the development of this culture. The horizons of Cuban society have been considerably widened by the relative increase in available information, the progressive broadening of access to the Internet, the greater

presence in Cuba of international NGOs and of cooperative intergovern-
mental projects in the areas of health, education, sports, and culture
abroad. In contrast, the politicization of "people to people" contacts, typi-
fied by the U.S. strategy of Track Two, has charged the atmosphere of
bilateral and international exchange considerably and has also inter-
fered, within Cuba, with critical and careful debate about some subjects.
In spite of that last phenomenon, however, culture has increasingly become the most dynamic realm of communication between the island
and the rest of the world.

These factors have promoted and affected, to various degrees, the development of a culture of debate in Cuba.

The motif of the three Cubans on a corner arguing over baseball represents a paradigm for debating ideas—not some arcane and marginal
discussion carried out by specialists. But the paradigm works only to the
extent that the debate takes place within its true context; in the baseball
example, this is the context of a transcendent national sport. Cuban social thought has been able to advance in a social environment that is not
resistant to a culture of debate. But further development of this culture
requires the gradual expansion of spaces, and this—as is generally the
case in the realm of culture, politics, and production of ideas—neither
occurs by decree nor can be promoted from outside.

The simplistic notion that political change comes only from outside
represents a point of convergence between some Cuban intellectuals living abroad and certain internal guardians of order; the former see it as
providential, the latter as a threat. Obviously, for a change to develop as a
living political process, it would have to be organically integrated in real
Cuban civil society, so that both civil society and the political system
could facilitate it and be transformed in the process.

Naturally, the right to speak about this process is not subject to the
geographical or political frontiers of the island. If we accept that Cuban
culture is not limited to these borders—as has been broadly recognized
in Cuba for the past ten years—we must admit that the debate over ideas
is not limited to the national territory either. Yet it would be wrong to
affirm, on the other hand, that all Cubans who hold forth about Cuba
from abroad are well-intentioned. I personally believe that much of the
reflection going on about Cuban problems ought to be known and discussed on the island, regardless of its provenance. But if the issue at

hand is the consolidation of liberties and participatory democracy, and the recovery or rescue of the Cuban project of social justice, development, equality, and independence under the adverse conditions of the transition, then the concrete steps, speeds, risks, and costs of this process can only play out in the historical space and time of real Cuban society. That is the primary reference point, the Aleph of this culture, where all the other Cubas converge. The same thing is true about any society with respect to its diaspora, however large.

This process, not confined to cultural or political elites, has its distinctive vibrations and intensities. In the end, the effort to make dialogue and debate prevail within and without does not delegitimize partisanship. And considering that we are dealing with three Cubans, it certainly does not imply discarding passion either.

Notes

Chapter 1. Introduction

This review by Jorge Luis Acanda González was originally published as "La mirada indiscreta o los riesgos de una ventana" in *Revolución y Cultura*, November–December 2000.

1. The Unión Nacional de Escritores y Artistas de Cuba (UNEAC) is the Writers' and Artists' Union referred to directly above. Among other books and periodicals, UNEAC publishes *La Gaceta de Cuba*, where several of the essays in this volume first appeared.—Trans.

2. The term *el quinquenio gris*, the Five Gray Years, is used semiofficially in Cuba to refer, in retrospect, to the period 1971–76 when government controls on arts and education were tightened and the range of what was considered revolutionary was narrowed.—Trans.

3. Armando Hart is a longtime Cuban revolutionary leader and high-ranking state official, minister of culture from 1976 to 1997, currently director of the program for study and dissemination of the works of José Martí.—Trans.

4. The reference is to an oft-cited remark in Fidel Castro's June 30, 1961, speech to intellectuals and artists who had expressed their fears of the coming of Soviet-style propagandistic art to Cuba. The speech, which also contains Castro's famous declaration "Inside the Revolution, everything; against the Revolution, nothing," has generally been reprinted under the title "Words to the Intellectuals."—Trans.

Chapter 2. Looking at Cuba: Notes toward a Discussion

This chapter, originally written in August 1993, appeared in *La Gaceta de Cuba*, September–October 1993.

1. I use "Cubanology" in a loose sense to refer to visions of Cuba, and not in the strictly academic sense. For an academic discussion see Nelson Valdés, "Revolution and Paradigms: A Critical Assessment of Cuban Studies," in *Cuban Political Economy: Controversies in Cubanology*, ed. Andrew Zimbalist (Boulder, Colo.: Westview Press, 1988).

2. For a differentiation between political culture and ideology, see Haroldo Dilla and Rafael Hernández, "Cultura política y participación en Cuba" [Political

culture and participation in Cuba], *Cuadernos de Nuestra América,* no. 15 (July–December 1990).

3. This subject has been avoided by Cubanology in a nearly systematic fashion. A look at the complete collection of the journal *Cuban Studies,* published for two decades by the University of Pittsburgh, will reveal that almost no one pays attention to the topic. Richard Fagen's pioneering work in *The Transformation of Political Culture in Cuba* (Stanford: Stanford University Press, 1969) continues to be a lone exception which has not been updated either empirically or theoretically.

4. References here and elsewhere in this article to "reformism," "autonomism," and "annexationism" have to do with the political legacy of tendencies during the Spanish colonial era that sought administrative or economic reforms within the imperial structure of Spain or the expansionist one of the United States, in opposition to proindependence forces.—Trans.

5. I share Cintio Vitier's outlook on the Eurocentrism implicit in this vision of intellectuals' exclusive role as culture's "critical conscience" in a confrontation with power, equidistant from all political positions, a vestal of some sterilized objectivity—as opposed to the intellectuals who, as in our Latin American case, act in history, with their criticism and their polemics, contributing to concrete social change and taking sides in favor of social justice and independence. See Cintio Vitier, "Resistencia y libertad" [Resistance and freedom] (Centro de Estudios Martianos, Havana, June 1992, mimeographed).

6. These figures are based on studies of legal emigration in the years 1990–92, which also report that 92 percent of these emigrants are white, more than 60 percent are from Havana City or Havana Province, 55 percent do not work (that is, they are students, housewives, retirees); 5.7 percent of all migrants of working age are unemployed. See Ernesto Rodríguez, "El patrón migratorio cubano: cambio y continuidad" [The Cuban migratory pattern: change and continuity], *Cuadernos de Nuestra América,* no. 18 (January–June 1992): 83–95.

7. See articles 14, 15, and 23 of the reformed Constitution. Subsequent references are also to this new version. For an objective analysis of the content of those changes, see Hugo Azcuy, "Aspectos de la ley de reforma constitucional cubana de 1992" [Aspects of the 1992 Cuban constitutional reform law] (Latin American Data Base, University of New Mexico, Albuquerque, August 1992, dossier).

8. Article 16.

9. Articles 1 and 3.

10. Articles 1 and 3.

11. Reforms expressed in chapter 9. In December 1992 a new electoral law was approved.

12. Article 5.

13. See the July 26 celebration speech by Fidel Castro in *Granma,* July 28, 1993, p. 3.

Chapter 3. Civil Society and Its Surroundings

This chapter first appeared in *La Gaceta de Cuba,* January–February 1994. The version translated here was lightly retouched by the author for the Cuban edition of this book, without changing any of the ideas of the original text.

1. Cristóbal's untitled text was published in the same issue of *La Gaceta de Cuba.*

2. Jorge G. Castañeda, *La utopía desarmada* (Mexico City: Joaquín Mortiz, 1993), 233 passim. The English version is *Utopia Unarmed: The Latin American Left after the Cold War* (New York: Knopf, 1993).

3. Jeffrey C. Isaac, "Civil Society and the Spirit of Revolt," *Dissent,* summer 1993, 358.

4. Carlos Marx, "Prólogo a la contribución a la crítica de la economia política" [Prologue to contribution to the criticism of political economy], in *Obras escogidas en tres tomos,* by C. Marx and F. Engels (Moscow: Progreso, 1976), 1:517.

5. Norberto Bobbio, "Sociedad civil" [Civil society], in *Diccionario de política,* by Norberto Bobbio and Nicola Matteucci (Madrid: Guadarrama, 1972), 1570–76.

6. Marx and Engels, "La ideología alemana" [The German ideology], in *Obras escogidas,* 1:39.

7. Marx, "Carta a P. Anenkov" [Letter to P. Anenkov], in *Selección de textos de Marx, Engels, y Lenin* (Havana: Pueblo y Educación, 1972), 2:169.

8. Engels, "Ludwig Feuerbach," in *Selección de textos,* 16.

9. Perry Anderson, *Las antinomias de Antonio Gramsci* [The antinomies of Antonio Gramsci], (Barcelona: Fontamara, 1978), 45–62.

10. "Society is one half of an antithetical pair whose other half is the state," says Immanuel Wallerstein in "World Systems Analysis," *Social Theory Today,* ed. Anthony Giddens (Stanford: Stanford University Press, 1978), 315.

11. Isaac, "Civil Society," 356–57.

12. I am not examining other Marxist authors such as Lenin or Bukharin or the bibliography of Latin American writers who have contributed to the diffusion of the concept in Continental social sciences; I have also refrained from reference to other significant theoretical aspects that go beyond the purpose of these pages.

13. In "Looking at Cuba" I do not exclude the state institutions of Cuban society, a quite peculiar idea. I recognize that, in that article, I use the term "society" a few times when I am referring to civil society, but I think it is clear in context. In any case, Cristóbal's precision is valid, even if I don't share all of his conclusions—in particular, that my imprecision is due to the influence of "some contemporary currents of thought" that he doesn't name.

14. In "Looking at Cuba" I discuss these paradoxical perceptions at length, although not as "paradoxes of Cuban reality" as Cristóbal states.

15. Damián Fernández, "Civil Society in Transition," in *Transition in Cuba: New Challenges for U.S. Policy,* ed. Lisandro Pérez (Miami: Cuban Research Institute, Florida International University, 1993), 100.

16. See chapter 2 under subhead "Cuban socialism consists of a political system . . ."

17. See its use by Fidel Castro in *History Will Absolve Me* and by Che Guevara in "Notes on the Ideology of the Cuban Revolution."

18. For a characterization of the sociostructural heterogeneity, see Mayra Espina, "Reproducción socioclasista en Cuba (período 1976–1988)" [Social class reproduction in Cuba, 1976–1988] (doctoral thesis, CIPS [Center for Psychological and Sociological Research], Havana, 1993).

19. A keen consciousness about this is summarized in the idea that "culture is the first thing that must be saved"; see "Fidel en el V Congreso de la UNEAC" [Fidel in the Fifth UNEAC Congress], *Granma*, November 25, 1993, p. 5.

20. Nor is there enough literature tackling that economic dimension itself in sufficient depth. See Julio Carranza, "Cuba: los retos de la economía" [Cuba: the challenge of the economy], *Cuadernos de Nuestra América*, no. 19 (July–December 1992): 141 passim.

21. There are an estimated 137,000 self-employed workers (J. A. Rodríguez, "El cuentapropista" [The self-employed], *Juventud Rebelde*, February 20, 1994, p. 4), and the total could reach 300,000 in 1994. According to some economists, in the course of the Special Period the black market may have grown more than twentyfold in monetary terms.

22. In "Looking at Cuba" I have tried to emphasize this trait of our political culture, indicating that criticism, disagreement, and demands are nothing but the children of the revolution itself at the level of civil society.

23. See the partial results of the study "La intelectualidad en el proyecto socialista cubano" [The intellectuals in the Cuban socialist project] (Havana: Equipo de Estructura Social, CIPS [Center for Psychological and Sociological Research], February 1993, typescript), 42.

24. Ibid., 45, 48.

25. These sources ground themselves particularly in the rising ideological profile of the Catholic hierarchy. See *El amor todo lo espera* [Love's hope is infinite], message of the Cuban conference of Catholic bishops, September 8, 1993.

26. Fernández, "Civil Society in Transition," 106.

27. Ibid., 131–43. This study lists some 106 organizations.

28. For a more extensive commentary on the relations between these two aspects and the problems of constructing a participatory democracy, see Haroldo Dilla and others published in *Participación popular y desarrollo en los municipios cubanos* [Popular participation and development in Cuban municipalities] (Havana: Center for the Study of the Americas, 1993), 140–47.

29. Fagen, *Transformation of Political Culture*, 10.

Chapter 4. The Second Death of Dogma: Notes on a Culture of the Left

This chapter originally appeared in *La Gaceta de Cuba*, September–October 1994.

1. Castañeda, *La utopía desarmada*, 105 passim, or *Utopia Unarmed*.

2. See the previous chapter for a broader discussion of the place of this concept in the history of ideas, and specifically of the theoretical implications of its use by Castañeda.

3. Supposedly. However, in practice, has the Belgian nation been fully constructed out of its Flemings and Walloons, or the Spanish one out of Basques, Catalans, and Castilians—not to speak of the case of the Croats and Serbs? And what shall we say about those diverse Northamericans who coexist in South Florida, whom some tend to identify as Jews, African Americans, Central Americans, and Cubans?

4. Guillermo O'Donnell, *El Estado burocrático-autoritario en América Latina* (Buenos Aires: Belgrano, 1982). In English as *Bureaucratic Authoritarianism: Argentina, 1966–1973, in Comparative Perspective,* trans. James McGuire and Rae Flory (Berkeley and Los Angeles: University of California Press, 1988).

5. José Martí, "Conferencia Monetaria de las Repúblicas de América" [Monetary Conference of the American Republics], in *Obras Completas* (Havana: Editorial Nacional de Cuba, 1962), 6:158.

6. On the historical necessity of American philosophical eclecticism (including that of Cuba), see Federico Álvarez, "Para una nueva lectura de la polémica cubana sobre el eclecticismo" [Toward a new reading of the Cuban debate on eclecticism], *Casa de las Américas,* no. 194 (January–March 1994): 75–84.

7. Castañeda, *La utopía desarmada,* 220.

8. It is striking that in *La utopía desarmada,* a book on the Latin American left and its battles, the policies of the United States receive so little attention. Even when it deals with Cuba, the book hardly mentions this subject.

9. For an expanded treatment of the missile crisis and its consequences, see Rafael Hernández, "Treinta días: las lecciones de la Crisis de Octubre y las relaciones cubanas con los EE.UU." [Thirty days: lessons from the October Crisis and Cuban relations with the U.S.], *Cuadernos de Nuestra América,* no. 16 (January–June 1991): 3–25.

10. The expression "importation of the Soviet model" should be taken with a grain of salt. A model of economic development or a political system is not the same as a barrel of petroleum or an industrial plant. In any case, the imitation of a model like that of "real socialism" involved the conscious decision to assume its presuppositions, its logic, and their implications.

11. An estimated half million students have graduated from Cuban universities in the revolutionary period. In the 1970s, 62 percent of the university graduates were of worker or peasant origin. In 1989, however, only 36 percent were sons and daughters of workers. In other words, the social origins of university professionals are increasingly tending to be professional families, which are the source of the majority of today's young intellectuals. See María Isabel Domínguez, "Las generaciones y la juventud: una reflexión sobre la sociedad cubana actual" [Generations and youth: a reflection on current Cuban society]

(doctoral thesis, CIPS [Center for Psychological and Sociological Research], Havana, 1993), 104.

12. According to the 1988 *Anuario Estadístico de Cuba,* professionals and technicians made up 21 percent of the active labor force. Rather than reducing the term "intellectual" to an occupational category (as opposed to "manual worker"), I prefer to identify it with the activity of specialists at the level of higher education and of creators who contribute to producing works of cultural value, whether works of art or of science, and to the generation and discussion of ideas. The issue of whether or not a political or institutional leader can be considered an "intellectual" is a casuistic one—although, in the majority of cases, such undifferentiated usage of the term can be confusing.

13. On the space for encounter and dialogue in UNEAC, see "Palabras de Abel Prieto en la inauguración del evento" [Abel Prieto's opening speech] in *"La cultura es lo primero que hay que salvar": Memorias del V Congreso de la UNEAC* (Havana: UNEAC, 1993), 13.

14. "La intelectualidad en el proyecto socialista cubano" [The intellectuals in the Cuban socialist project] (Havana: Equipo de Estructura Social, CIPS [Center for Psychological and Sociological Research], February 1993, typescript), 42.

15. Ibid., 46. This vocation for international interchange has been a strategic one in the national self-consciousness since José Martí warned Cubans of the danger of the "conceited villager [who thinks] his village is the whole world"; see "Nuestra América" in Martí, *Obras Completas,* 6:15.

16. The critique of "unanimism" begins with the Call to the Fourth Congress of the Cuban Communist Party, 1990. For discussion of the distorted conceptions of unity in "real socialism," see Jorge Luis Acanda, "Gramsci y la Revolución Cubana" [Gramsci and the Cuban Revolution], *Revolución y Cultura,* September–October 1993, 8.

17. See "Presencia y funciones de la cultura cubana en las circunstancias actuales" [Presence and role of Cuban culture in the current circumstances] in *Memorias del V Congreso de la UNEAC,* 13.

18. Research on youth reveals, however, that among them the intellectuals are the group reflecting the highest social values. See Domínguez, "Las generaciones y la juventud," 111. See also *La cultura cubana de hoy: temas para un debate* [Cuban culture today: issues for debate] (document approved by the National Council of UNEAC, May 26, 1992), 5–7.

19. Ibid.

20. Isaac Deutscher, "The Ex-Communist's Conscience," in *Heretics and Renegades* (London: Jonathan Cape, 1969), 15.

21. Ibid.

22. Apart from its academic use, this term has a European ideological history that dates from the origin of the Cold War and is now being renewed and extended on the Old Continent in a dangerous way. See Maurice Agulhon, "Faut-il

reviser l'histoire de l'antifascisme?" [Should the history of antifascism be revised?], *Le Monde Diplomatique*, June 1994, 17.

23. This not only has compromised the development of Marxist thought and of social science but has also limited several generations' ability to think. For a critique from the point of view of these generations, see Domínguez, "Las generaciones y la juventud," 149, and Acanda, "Gramsci y la Revolución Cubana," 6.

24. Fundamentalists speak of a "true socialism" which has come into existence only in monstrous forms, not the way it appears in books. In their zeal to erase "real socialism" from history, some "ex-dogmatics" end up erasing the real history of socialism at a single stroke.

25. "Marxist-Leninist thinking, Engel's thinking, Che's thinking have a permanent validity as long as they are not seen as immutable dogmas. . . . No theoretician's or political figure's thought should be taken as something inflexible, something dogmatic. . . . We have to avoid converting the thinking of the most illustrious political figures, the most eminent revolutionaries, into dogma—because, among other things, every thought arises out of a particular moment," said Fidel Castro in *Un grano de maíz: Conversación con Tomás Borge* (Mexico City: Fondo de Cultura Económica, 1992), 85; in English as *Face to Face with Fidel Castro: A Conversation with Tomás Borge,* trans. Mary Todd (Melbourne, Australia: Ocean Press, 1993).

26. See *Memorias del V Congreso de la UNEAC,* 13.

27. As George H. Sabine, in *A History of Political Theory,* 3d ed. (New York: Holt, Rinehart and Winston, 1961), 736–37, says in discussing nineteenth-century England, conservatism "had publicized itself as the protector of stability and security against too rapid and too drastic change, the principal cause of change being the expansion of trade and industry which was a typical policy of liberalism."

28. *Memorias del V Congreso de la UNEAC,* 11.

29. ". . . finding new forms of appeal and new spaces for dialogue, with a language devoid of stereotypes, capable of putting forth the arguments of the Cuban Revolution in a creative way" (ibid., 29).

30. *La cultura cubana de hoy,* 4.

31. For a problematizing treatment, see Haroldo Dilla, "Cuba: la crisis y la rearticulación del consenso político (notas para un debate socialista), *Cuadernos de Nuestra América,* no. 20 (July–December 1993): 20–45.

32. "Fidel en el V Congreso de la UNEAC," in *Memorias del V Congreso de la UNEAC,* 6.

33. Following Gramsci, I am contraposing "common sense" to "good sense." To contrast the discourse of "common sense" with the critical rationality of "good sense" may be more productive than the use of other dichotomies such as "instrumental" versus "emancipatory." For viewpoints on the latter, see the interesting

debate among Rafael Rojas, Cintio Vitier, and Arturo Arango in *Casa,* no. 194 (January–March 1994): 85–113.

34. In a text entitled "Grandeza y miseria de la utopía cubana," Jesús Díaz claims that the only alternative for Cuba's future must begin from the idea that the United States would completely cease to be hostile to Cuba's independence and sovereignty and "would unconditionally retreat" from its current positions. This reasoning converges with the view of those in Cuba who insist it is impossible to move forward even an inch in the democratization of the political system as long as the hostility of the United States continues.

Chapter 5. Civil Society and Politics in the 1990s

This chapter was originally a presentation at the Cuban Foreign Ministry's Higher Institute of Foreign Relations in Havana on March 7, 1995.

1. See the basic works of Fernando Ortíz or the ethnologic studies and descriptions of Lydia Cabrera published before 1959.

2. The Summit of the Americas, held in Miami on December 9–11, 1994, issued a *Declaration of Principles,* available at www.summit-americas.org/miamidec.htm, and a *Plan of Action,* available at www.summit-americas.org/miamiplan.htm, from which the quotes that follow are taken.

3. *Plan of Action,* part 1, section 1, "Strengthening Democracy."

4. *Plan of Action,* part 1, section 2, "Promoting and Protecting Human Rights."

5. *Plan of Action,* part 1, section 3, "Invigorating Society/Community Participation."

6. *Plan of Action,* part 1, section 1. Cuban emigres in the hemisphere are held hostage by these circumstances. The positions of the U.S. government and some Latin American governments and international political organizations have privileged the elitist and intransigent sector of the emigrant population, which represents the upper class and annexationist tendencies. The great majority of emigres do not enjoy truly democratic representation. For a more extended treatment, see Rafael Hernández, "Sobre las relaciones con la comunidad cubana en los EE.UU." [On relations with the Cuban community in the U.S.], *Cuba en el Mes* (Latin American Data Base, Center for the Study of the Americas, University of New Mexico, Albuquerque), April 1994.

7. Fidel Castro, speech at the Fourth Ibero-American Summit, Cartagena, in *Granma,* July 15, 1994.

8. Ibid.

Chapter 6. Toward a New Socialist Society?: Changes, Crisis, and Social Configurations in Cuba

This chapter was originally published in *Nueva Sociedad* (Venezuela), no. 157 (September–October 1998).

1. Fidel Castro, *Por el camino correcto* [On the right path] (Havana: Editora Política, 1988).

2. Fidel Castro, *Informe Central al III Congreso del PCC* [Main report to the third congress of the Cuban Communist Party] (Havana: Editora Política, 1986).

3. See articles 14, 15, and 23 of the revised Constitution. For an analysis, see Hugo Azcuy, "Aspectos de la ley de reforma constitucional cubana de 1992" [Aspects of the 1992 Cuban constitutional reform law] (Latin American Data Base, University of New Mexico, Albuquerque, August 1992, dossier).

4. The assemblies of People's Power are the elected local, provincial, and national legislatures. Their elected members run on personal reputation rather than programmatic platforms. Nomination and election mechanisms are discussed below.—Trans.

5. According to the 1988 *Anuario Estadístico,* professionals and technicians made up 21 percent of the active workforce.

6. It is estimated that some two thousand associations are entered in the Ministry of Justice's national registry. These range from, for instance, the Yoruba Society of Cuba to the Association of Catholic Journalists.

7. In the classical vision of Antonio Gramsci, those ideological structures are strict components of civil society. For a reflection on this concept and its application to current Cuban society, see Jorge Luis Acanda, "Sociedad civil y hegemonía" [Civil society and hegemony], *Temas,* no. 6 (April–June 1996).

8. Consuelo Martín, Maricela Perera, and Maiky Díaz, "La vida cotidiana en Cuba: Una mirada psicosocial" [Daily life in Cuba: A psychosocial view], *Temas,* no. 7 (July–September 1996).

9. Rafael Hernández, "1999: La lógica democrática y el futuro de las relaciones entre los Estados Unidos y Cuba" [1999: The logic of democracy and the future of relations between the United States and Cuba], in *La democrácia en Cuba y el diferendo con los Estados Unidos* [Democracy in Cuba and the Differendum with the United States], ed. Haroldo Dilla (Havana: Ediciones CEA, 1995).

10. See articles 1 and 3 of the text of the reformed Constitution.

11. See article 8. For an analytic commentary, see Azcuy, "Aspectos de la ley."

12. Reforms expressed in chapter 9 of the Constitution.

13. To identify it as an authoritarian, Bonapartist, or "really existing socialist" regime (in the style of the military dictatorships of Brazil or Chile, the Franco regime in Spain, or the "people's democracies" of Eastern Europe) lacks not only historical basis but explanatory value as to what is happening—and may happen—in Cuba.

14. Hernández, "1999."

15. Monetary transfers to specific projects totaled about fifty million dollars in the period 1990–96, and were growing. This aid has gone especially to base communities and the most vulnerable sections of the population. See *Cooperación para el desarrollo entre ONGs europeas y cubanas* [Cooperation for development among European and Cuban NGOs] (Havana: Centro de Estudios Europeos, 1996), resulting from a meeting of European and Cuban NGOs in Brussels in March 1996.

16. "Ayuda y socorro." This includes aid in the areas of food, medicine, water treatment, education, renewable energy, environment, housing, the disabled, women, human resources, employment, and the development of Cuban NGOs as such. The list of major contributors in 1994 included Bread for the World, Catholic Relief Service, Caritas (in various countries), Misereor–Campaign against Hunger and Disease in the World, and Oxfam. See *Cooperación para el desarrollo: Cuba, Informe 1994* (Havana: United Nations Development Program, 1995), 35–37, 15 ("Desembolsos de la Asistencia de ONGs por sectores").

17. *Cooperación para el desarrollo entre ONGs europeas y cubanas.*

18. The ACS links several differentiated segments, such as Caricom, Central America, the large coastal nations—Mexico, Venezuela, and Colombia—and some states that are part of other international organizations, such as Haiti, the Dominican Republic, and Cuba. The association is composed of twenty-four countries, with the illustrious exception of the United States.

19. Hugo Azcuy, "Los derechos humanos en las relaciones interamericanas" [Human rights in inter-American relations], in *Cuba en las Américas,* ed. Rafael Hernández (Havana: Centro de Estudios sobre América/Instituto de Estudios Políticos de América Latina, 1994).

20. Juan Valdés Paz, "El sistema político cubano" [The Cuban political system], in *Cuba en las Américas,* ed. Hernández.

21. Rafael Hernández, "Las relaciones con los Estados Unidos" [Relations with the United States], in *Cuba en las Américas,* ed. Hernández.

Chapter 7. On Discourse

This chapter originally appeared in *La Gaceta de Cuba,* January–March 1999.

1. John B. Thompson, *Studies in the Theory of Ideology* (Berkeley and Los Angeles: University of California Press, 1984), 8.

2. Adam Schaff, *Language and Cognition,* ed. Robert S. Cohen, trans. Olgierd Wojtasiewicz (New York: McGraw-Hill, 1973).

3. Pierre Bourdieu, *Ce que parler veut dire: l'économie des échanges linguistiques* (Paris: Fayard, 1981). In English as *Language and Symbolic Power,* ed. John B. Thompson, trans. Gino Raymond and Matthew Adamson (Cambridge: Harvard University Press, 1991).

4. Carlos Paz, in *Diccionario cubano de términos vulgares y populares* [Cuban dictionary of vulgar and popular speech] (Havana: Ciencias Sociales, 1994), 6, 8.

5. Carlos J. Moneta, "La dimension cultural de la globalización" [The cultural dimension of globalization], *Capítulos del SELA,* no. 45 (January–February 1996).

6. A *shopping* is a store selling goods for U.S. dollars; a *paladar,* literally "palate," is a private, family-run restaurant; a *jinetera,* literally "one who jockeys," sells companionship or sex to tourists; a *maceta,* literally "flowerpot," is one who has accumulated money through black market activities. To "escape" (*escapar*) is to survive by bending the rules; "Stub out the cigar!" (*¡Apaga el tabaco!*) means "Quit

talking nonsense!"; *librar* (literally, to get free of some encumbrance) is a slangier version of *escapar*, rather like the U.S. "get away with."—Trans.

7. In the 1960s and early 1970s, those on one side of this controversy held that revolutionary Cuban literature and art needed to capture the starkness and violence of the confrontation between pro- and counterrevolutionary groups and to reflect the "real speech" of the people. Those on the other side held that the new literature and art should present a model of "proper" culture for the uplift of the people, especially of the new generations.—Trans.

8. Francois Rabelais, *Gargantua and Pantagruel*, book 4, chapters 60–61.

9. Abel Prieto, *El humor de Misha: la crisis del "socialismo real" en el chiste político* [The humor of Misha: the crisis of "real socialism" in the political joke] (Buenos Aires: Colihue, 1997).

10. Report of the Political Bureau on the country's political and social situation, approved at the Fifth Plenum of the Central Committee of the Cuban Communist Party, March 23, 1996, as reported in *Granma*, March 26, 1996, p. 5.

11. L. Onikov and N. Shishlin, *Breve diccionario político* [Brief political dictionary], trans. O. Razinkov (Moscow: Progreso, 1983). In another dictionary, Nicolás Abbagnano cites an amusing definition of dogmatism attributed to none less than Emmanuel Kant: "Poor reasoning about things which are not understood and about which no one in the world will ever understand anything."

12. As Abel Prieto has pointed out in *El humor de Misha*, where a new socialist culture could have been born and developed, "something broke down, and the consensus eroded among all sorts of errors and deformations, leaving a false and rootless 'culture' more and more divorced from the experience and feelings of the majority."

Chapter 8. Three Cubans Talking Baseball: Political Culture, Ideological Debate, and Civil Society in Cuba

This chapter originally appeared in *Nexos* (Mexico City), winter 2001.

1. The distinction in Spanish is between the verbs *disentir* and *disidir*, which come from different Latin roots, as do the nouns "dissent" and "dissidence" in English. The former root means to feel differently; the latter one means to sit apart.—Trans.

Rafael Hernández is the editor of *Temas*, the leading Cuban magazine in the social sciences and the humanities, which is renowned for its contribution to intellectual controversy on the island. He is a senior research fellow at the Centro de Investigación de la Cultura Cubana Juan Marinello in Havana and is the author or editor of several books, including *United States–Cuban Relations in the Nineties* (1989) and *Cuba and the Caribbean* (1997).

Dick Cluster, lecturer at the University of Massachusetts, Boston, has translated a variety of Cuban literary figures including Abel Prieto, Pedro de Jesús, Mirta Yáñez, Aida Bahr, Mylene Fernández, and Antonio José Ponte. He is the author of novels and historical works including *They Should Have Served That Cup of Coffee.*